# How to Plant SONflowers

by Tonja K. Taylor

HOW TO PLANT SONFLOWERS

**First edition. July 26, 2025.**

Copyright © 2025 Tonja K. Taylor.

ISBN: 978-1965641422

Written by Tonja K. Taylor.

# Also by Tonja K. Taylor

**The Adventures of Princess Pearl, P.O.W.E.R. Girl!**
The Adventures of Princess Pearl, P.O.W.E.R. Girl!
The Adventures of Princess Pearl, P.O.W.E.R. Girl! Book III
The Adventures of Princess Pearl, P.O.W.E.R. Girl! Book IV
The Adventures of Princess Pearl, P.O.W.E.R. Girl! Book V

**Standalone**
POWERLight Lit Tips for Better Teaching
The New Legacy Expanded
P.O.W.E.R. Princess Poetry Plus
The Adventures of Princess Pearl, P.O.W.E.R. Girl!
Your Holy Health: Effective Secrets to Divine Life
Spirit Songs & Stories Enhanced
Spirit Songs & Stories #2
Visions of the King: Jesus Revealed
How to Plant SONFlowers

Watch for more at https://www.faithwriters.com/ member-profile.php?id=64826.

# Table of Contents

*How to Plant SONflowers* devotional. Most works previously published 2006 on www.Cfaith.com[1], and/or on the website FaithWriters.com. First book printing in 2017 by Tonja K. Taylor. Revised and republished 2025, by POWERLight Learning, Fort Worth, Texas. Cover by Madeline Dietze. Editing help by Clayton Taylor and Victoria.

POWERLight Learning, *"Because what you read matters!"*

Proverbs 4:23 (Berean Standard Bible) says: **"Guard your heart with all diligence, for from it flows springs of life."**

Romans 12:2 says: **"Do not be conformed to this world, but be transformed by the renewing of your mind. Then you will be able to test and approve what is the good, pleasing, and perfect will of God."** (Berean Standard Bible)

Scripture quotations taken from the Berean Standard Bible or Amplified Classic Bible (AMPC).

**Read over 1,500 free** insightful, helpful, and sometimes humorous articles, stories, and/or songs on Tonja's site at FaithWriters.com: https://www.faithwriters.com/member-profile.php?id=64826

Check out our **300+ videos** on various helpful subjects at our **"River Rain Creative" You Tube** channel.

Also, listen to our **more-than-40** of our **"RainWater"** podcasts from 2019 **on Spotify.** (Includes an **excerpt of Book One of The Adventures of Princess Pearl, P.O.W.E.R. Girl!; a Hebrew blessing;** and some **Spanish** phrases.)

---

1.    http://www.Cfaith.com

# How to Plant SONflowers

I bet you like flowers. I do. I think they are one of the most beautiful things on earth.

They pop up out of the barren winter ground, and sprinkle lovely bits of color everywhere. Many of them smell so sweet.

Only God can make a flower, and I know that He in His loving wisdom gave them to us humans to delight us. He is so wonderful!

But how are flowers made? From a seed. And not just flowers! Everything you see came from a seed, including you!

Even man-made things like buildings and machines and cars came from a seed—the seed of an idea.

Flowers happen the same way. God gives the seed, and the seed is planted in the ground, then given water and sunshine and food. Only then can it grow and produce that beautiful bloom!

The seed would still be a seed if it stayed above ground, but it would never become what God meant it to be, would it? It must be planted, or "sowed." Then once it is sowed, it will start to produce what is inside.

It is the same with our lives. What are they producing? Are our lives like beautiful flower gardens, full of lovely, sweet-smelling flowers of love and peace and joy and energy and direction and faith in our loving Daddy God?

I call these and other good seeds that we plant to produce godly traits "SONflowers." I call them SONflowers because Jesus is the Son of God, and God planted Jesus the Son in the ground after He died on the cross for us, to produce a huge family of children—SONflowers!—just like Jesus!

**For those God foreknew, He also predestined to be conformed to the image of His Son, so that He would be the firstborn among many brothers.** - Rom. 8:29

Then, three days later, Jesus, the Rose of Sharon, the most beautiful SONflower of all, arose from the ground to live forever! Hallelujah!

And He wants to help you plant SONflowers in all the people you know. If you have accepted Jesus the Son into your heart as your Savior, then you have His Holy Spirit living in you, and it's really Him planting SONflowers through you into other people. Totally cool!

It's easy and fun to plant SONflowers. The very best way, of course, is to plant the Word of God, which are the most excellent SONflower seeds. We do this by reading and learning God's Word, and living it.

And when we live God's Word—when we live like His Holy Bible says to live—then we plant SONflower seeds into other people, because they see us be like Jesus, and they learn more about how loving and wise and exciting He is. They see the benefits of living right. They want to be like Him.

And that is why we plant SONflowers! Sure, every flower starts with a seed. Everything starts with a seed, including the Kingdom of Heaven (Matt. 13:31).

Our words are seeds. Our actions are seeds. It is our job to plant only good seeds, so the best way to plant good seeds, and especially SONflowers, is to base our lives and our speech on the Word of God (Gal. 6:7).

Jesus says in Isaiah 55:11: **"...so My word that proceeds from My mouth will not return to Me empty, but it will accomplish what I please, and it will prosper where I send it."**

When we plant SONflowers, we will get—or "reap"—SONflowers. We may not get to see all of those lovely blossoms, but our Father Who is faithful and Who tends all of His SONflower gardens will count them all—and reward us for them!

*Ask your Father in Heaven how you can purposely plant special SONflowers today!!*

# How to Have God as Your Best Friend

Jesus Christ the Messiah, the Anointed One, the King of kings and LORD of lords, will be coming back to get all who have believed in Him, to take them back to Heaven to live with Him forever (Revelation 22:12)!

He wants to be your BIFF—your Best Invisible Friend Forever—and take you with Him to Paradise.

In Paradise, or Heaven where God the Father and Jesus the Son always are, there is freedom and joy and plenty of every good and beautiful thing.

In Heaven, there are no bad things, no darkness at all. In Heaven, there is only the glorious goodness and light and love of the LORD! God and Jesus are eager for you to come live with them after your life on earth.

When your body dies, they want you to live with them in Heaven. The holy angels, and all the other people who died that love Jesus are there.

Some people think that, once a person's body dies, they stop living. It is true that the body does not come back to life, unless the LORD brings it to life again.

Your spirit, the life of God within you—the real you—is eternal! Your spirit, which came out of God (John 1:1-3), lives forever!

So the real you is a spirit, and your body is just a container to hold your spirit while you are on earth; like an astronaut needs a space suit to live in space.

When a person's body dies, the spirit within that person immediately leaves the body and goes up or down—to Heaven, to live with God forever, or to hell, to be tormented by the devil our enemy forever.

This is absolute, meaning this is the way it is, and this is the way it will always be, no matter what any person says.

So you have a choice; you can choose to serve and live with Jesus in the most wonderful life you can imagine, or choose to serve and live a horrible, tormented life with the devil, who hates God, and who hates you. But God loves you, and every good thing in your life is from Him!

He loves you so much that He sent His only Son, Jesus (the King!), to shed every drop of His pure blood to pay the sin debt every one of us owed, and to die for us, because He wanted us to be free to love Him and live with Him now and forever, and to help other people know how good He is!

Yes, Jesus Christ was God Who chose to become a Man; born of the virgin Mary, and He lived on earth as a human, like the rest of us. Then, at the age of 30, the LORD baptized Him in water and in the Holy Spirit, after which the LORD tested Him in the wilderness for 40 days. Then He officially started His ministry.

After three and a half years, He was wrongfully condemned by the Jews, crucified by the Romans, forgave the world while hanging on the cross, committed His spirit to the Father—then died.

After three days of being dead, He was resurrected by the power of God! Even His disciples didn't believe it at first, but He stayed on earth for 40 days, and was seen alive again by hundreds of people.

Then He ascended to Heaven, where He sits and reigns at the right hand of the Father, praying for us as the High Priest before Jehovah.

But He did not leave us by ourselves; He sent the wonderful Holy Spirit, so that, instead of Jesus being only one place at a time, the Spirit of the LORD is now everywhere at once, and able to live in the hearts of all of us who believe in Him!

Hallelujah!

All of us have done something wrong, broken one rule of God or another.

We can never be good enough nor do enough good things to get to Heaven (Romans 3:21-26, Ephesians 2:1-10).

So, just to say it another way and be clear, Jesus, the perfect Son of God Who did nothing wrong, took everything you and I have ever done wrong and paid the debt of sin by spilling His blood for us on the cross (John 3:15-17)!

He wanted us to have the chance to be with Him forever in Heaven, and to enjoy getting to know Him here on earth.

Instead of us dying to pay for our sins (which we could never truly do anyway!), Jesus did it for us, because He loves us that much. He was crucified on a cross—the worst death anyone could die—and after three days, He came back to life (Matthew 28:6)!

Now He lives forever in Heaven, praying for us, helping us, loving us, and waiting for us to work with Him (Romans 8:34).

Once we ask Jesus to forgive us of our sins and come to live by His Holy Spirit in our hearts, God the Heavenly Father adopts us as His child! Jesus becomes our Savior, our Brother, and our Best Invisible Friend Forever. Jesus brings us joy, peace, love, wisdom, and every good thing.

Once He comes to live with us, He is with us always (Matthew 28:20). No matter what any other person on earth does, Jesus will forever love us and be with us!

None of us can get into Heaven to live with God the Father, Who is perfect and holy, unless we first become friends with His Son Jesus Christ (the Anointed One and His Anointing).

He constantly talks to the Father about us. Christ is our connection to the Holy God of Heaven. Being friends with Jesus starts in our live now on earth, because once a person's body dies, it is too late for them to choose Him.

Jesus the King of all is coming back very soon to get all of us who love Him, to take us out of this crazy world so we can be safe and happy and healed and have everything we need and want, in the wonderful life with God.

He will reward us for how we have lived for Him (Revelation 22:12).

Although He loves every person He ever created, He will only take with Him to Heaven those who have truly received Him as Savior (Matthew 7:23).

If you would like to go to Heaven and have God as your loving Father and Jesus as your BIFF, and start enjoying the best life you could ever have today, just say this prayer:

<u>Dear Jesus, Please forgive me of everything I've done wrong and come into my heart and be my LORD and Savior and Friend! Help me get to know You and teach me through Your Word how to love and obey You, for You are the true King Who rules! And thank You for loving me so much. Thank You for saving me and helping me to enjoy and love You! In Your Name, amen!</u>

Romans 10:13 says "All who call upon the Name of the LORD shall be saved." If you prayed this prayer, a miracle just happened! You became alive in Christ! Your spirit became new, and the Spirit of Jesus just came into your heart to help you live a wonderful life—as a new person!

**Therefore if anyone is in Christ, he is a new creation. The old has passed away. Behold, the new has come!** – 2 Cor. 5:17, Berean Standard Bible

The Holy Spirit also came and put a Heavenly mark on you to tell God and the angels and the devil and everyone else that you now belong to Jesus (Ephesians 1:13, 2 Timothy 2:19)!

He will love and help you forever. Now Jesus and His angels are having a party, celebrating your wonderful decision to become part God's family!

Now, the way to learn all about your new Best Invisible Friend Forever is to read your Bible—His special Letter to you—His new dear friend!

*Ask Him to show you the church family you need to meet with, to learn even more about Him and have other Christians to pray with you, and help you know wonderful it is to live with Him!*

<u>Welcome to the Royal Family—the best life you could ever have!</u>

# 16 Ways to Not Be Bored Reading the Bible

U ntil now you have not asked for asked for anything in My name. Ask and you will receive, so that your joy may be complete.—John 16:24, Berean Study Bible

Sometimes we need to do something different to help us be more interested in what we should be interested in—like reading the Bible! Here are a few things that have worked for me and others, to renew our devotion to fellowshipping with God in His Word every day.

Here are just a few things I've done, and/or others have done, to keep our interest in the vital Word of God every day:

1. Read online

2. Read in a different language, next to your language, and compare

3. Listen online in your language

4. Listen online in another language, with subtitles in your language

5. Listen to videos of Bible-based preaching

6. Set the audio read feature on your phone in the Bible applications you can download

7. Ask the LORD where to start reading, aside from any daily schedule

8. Ask the LORD to lead you to just one Scripture you need right now, and write it out on notecards, then post them on your mirrors, refrigerator, office walls, kitchen cabinets, and anywhere else you want to see them

9. Read the same Scripture in several different versions.

10. Buy Scripture cards at a local store, and put them different places, and/or shuffle them, to read a different one every day—or several times a day!

11. Choose favorite Scriptures, and illustrate them, or have your kids draw pictures to go with them, like I did for my daughter in her 6 and 7 grades during homeschool.

12. Do a keyword search, such as "power" or "love" or "truth" or "peace" or "joy" or "marriage" or "children" or whatever you want, and you'll be amazed at the Scriptures that address that topic.

13. Write out a Scripture (or many) on paper, especially on card stock or paper that's stiffer than regular notebook paper, and then cut up the Scripture into one card per word. Shuffle the cards, and practice till you can put it in order, including the Scripture reference. This is a great game for kids at church, VBS, Scripture memory clubs, or anywhere—including for adult kids!

14. Open the Bible at "random" and point to a Scripture, and ask the LORD to speak to your heart about it (It may take a few minutes, hours, or days...weeks...but HE WILL!).

15. Bible board games.

16. Bible online games and apps.

I'm sure there are more ways, for God is Elohim, the Creator, Who knows all things. Ask Him!

Have fun, for the LORD Jesus delights in you delighting in Him and His Word!

He is coming very soon, and the more of His Word you know, the better your life will be, and the more prepared you will be—and the more you can help others be prepared—for His return!

**Behold, I am coming soon, and My reward is with Me, to give to each one according to what he has done.** —Revelation 22:12, Berean Study Bible

*Ask the LORD to show you even more ways you can have fun learning His Word. He'll help you!*

# Some Scriptures to Pray for Your Pastors

It is a form of love and humility to pray, especially for other people. When we pray, we are asking the LORD to get involved in specific ways in our lives and others', and He hears and answers our earnest prayers!

The LORD prompts me very often to pray for my pastors, and early this morning, He gave me specific Scriptures to pray for them. I will share them below with you.

Whether they are the head pastors, youth pastors, childrens' pastors, or any other person bearing the title of "pastor", they have very important responsibilities, and pray for us and watch over our souls (Hebrews 13:17).

So when we pray for them, and especially speak the Word of God over them, it strengthens them, gives them grace to do their work with even greater dedication and satisfaction, and helps them be in greater unity and understanding with the groups they lead.

Speaking the Word over others and ourselves always causes a positive reaction—although it may be unseen for a while—for the Word of God is always at work (Isaiah 55:10-11), accomplishing His perfect will in the earth!

The LORD has chosen to limit Himself, overall, to His actions being a response to our faith-filled prayers. What an honor and privilege and responsibility we have—to affect the course of things and people in the earth, with our words!

I'm so glad the LORD taught me to "personalize" the Scriptures, for most of the verses in the Bible can be applied to one's own life, and the lives of those we cover.

Praying for any spiritual leader in the earth is good, but praying for one's own pastor(s) is even more targeted.

First, start off by thanking the LORD for your pastors. They are gifts to the church body! (I have personalized these and the following in this writing.) I Thessalonians 5:12-13 is a good place to start.

You can say: "Thank You, Father, as You say in I Thessalonians 5:12 and 13 (AMPC), 12 **"we know and thank You for our pastors, who labor among us [We recognize them for what they are, acknowledge and appreciate and respect them all]—our leaders who are over us in the Lord and those who warn and kindly reprove and exhort us. 13 And we hold them in very high and most affectionate esteem in [intelligent and sympathetic] appreciation of their work. We are at peace among ourselves."**

To personalize the Scriptures, you can put your pastors' names there, and put it in the present tense. For instance, you can take Colossians 4:12 (AMPC) and do that: **"[I am] always striving for Pastor (name(s)) earnestly in my prayers, [pleading] that he/they may [as persons of ripe character and clear conviction] stand firm and mature [in spiritual growth], convinced and fully assured in everything willed by God."**

You can say: "Thank You, Father, as You say in Ephesians 1:15-17 (Berean Standard Bible): we praise You that we, **"having heard of the faith in the Lord Jesus which *exists* among (our pastors and their) love for all the saints, (we) do not cease giving thanks (for them), while making mention *of (them)* in (our) prayers; that the God of our Lord Jesus Christ, the Father of glory, may give to (them) a spirit of wisdom and of revelation in the knowledge of Him."** (parenthetical pronouns mine)

So we can put our pastor's name(s) in these Scriptures, and say "So, Father God, we thank You that You are giving them (your pastor(s) name(s) here) endless energy and boundless strength in doing Your will!"

Then you can keep going—for you can never speak too much of the Word of God. Not only are you blessing your pastors (and thus their families, and yourself and all those whom that pastor or those pastors lead, but you are sowing the living, life-giving Word of God into your own heart and life directly, as you see and hear it!

The possibilities are almost endless of how you can—especially when you ask the LORD to lead you to just the right Scriptures for your pastor(s)—pray the Word for your leaders!

Here is another excellent one: (You can say), "Father, all of Psalm 119 is excellent, for every one of us, Your people. For our pastors, we pray Psalm 119, especially verse 1, which says **'Blessed (happy, fortunate, to be envied) are our pastor(s) the undefiled (the upright, truly sincere, and blameless) in the way [of the revealed will of God], who walk (order their conduct and conversation) in the law of the Lord (the whole of God's revealed will)'"** (AMPC version).

You can just stop and praise the LORD personally for the goodness and faithfulness and obedience (and often, sacrifice) of your pastor(s), with expressions like, "Thank You, Daddy God, for giving us pastor(s) that are so devoted to you, and to us; who want to do their very best, to help us know You more, and to bring You glory in every way!"

You can start or end (or both!) your prayers with words such as, "Thank You that as You say in You say in I John 5:14-15, that I know that I have what I ask, because I pray in Your will and know that You hear me. Hallelujah! So I ask all of these things for our pastor(s), in the glorious, victorious, all-powerful Name of Jesus Christ, the King, and thank You!"

God knows all things, and He knows when we are sincere. He knows when we are really honoring Him, or not. However, His Love for us, His kids (once we have truly received Christ Jesus as our Savior and LORD, by asking His forgiveness of our sins and inviting Jesus to be the center of our lives) far supersedes anything else.

As we pray, we cannot go by feelings, for we may not *feel* like we really mean what we say; we may not *feel* like we are really in faith; we may not *feel* like us speaking God's Word is really doing anything.

*But it is!* As God writes to us in Isaiah 55:10-11: **"For as the rain and the snow come down from heaven, And do not return there without watering the earth And making it bear and sprout, And furnishing seed to the sower and bread to the eater; So will My word be which goes forth from My mouth; It will not return to Me empty, Without accomplishing what I desire, And without succeeding *in the matter* for which I sent it."** (Berean Standard Bible)

Hallelujah!

Faith—trusting God—is not a feeling. Thank goodness! Faith is a decision. We decide to believe God and what He tells us in His Word, for He can never lie! Hallelujah! He wouldn't even if He could! He *is* integrity and faithfulness and everything right. He is The Way, the Truth, and the Life. Hallelujah!

Also, the Holy Spirit, the Spirit of Christ Jesus, is the One Who really prays through us and is talking to the Father (while using our words, and our decisions to partner with Him, to get His will done in the earth to strengthen and help our pastor(s), and others. It's a wonderful win-win!). He inspires us on what to pray, and brings our pastor(s) to our thoughts, to remind us to pray for them—for sometimes they may need us to pray for them in the middle of the night, or at a time different than we normally pray for them.

When we do pray for our pastor(s) and/or others, it is always a form of love; of giving; of service to the LORD and them, and we always benefit, as is stated in James 5:16 (Berean Standard Bible): **"Therefore confess your sins to each other and pray for each other**

**so that you may be healed. The prayer of a righteous man has great power to prevail."**

What an honor and privilege to come before the God of Heaven and earth and have a personal audience with Him; to be heard and answered by Him! He is such a personal, amazing, darling Father God!

If you like, you can pray Scriptures for your pastor(s) as you pray for others. The Word of God is for everyone, praise Him

After all, we are—as true Believers in what the LORD Jesus Christ did for us on the cross by shedding His blood to pay for our sins and give us eternal life, Hallelujah!—all in the same Royal Family of God.

If you don't have a current pastor, pray for pastors and other spiritual leaders around the world. They need it!

Also ask the LORD where your Bible-believing church is, for you need—especially in these strange and turbulent times of the Last Days of earth!—to be part of a body, to have a leader that God put in place, to pray for you (Heb. 10:25).

The spiritual covering and loving care that true pastors carry is very important—and can even make a difference in the life or death of people in their church (but only to a point. We are each ultimately responsible for our relationship with God, and thus our obedience to Him. God gave us all a few will, and not even He will violate it.) Pastors are vessels to help encourage and strengthen you, and help you in other ways.

If there are no Bible-believing churches in your area, then you can find an online church that meets at least weekly, and that truly preaches and teaches the Word of God.

Spread the news: King Jesus is coming soon! Hallelujah!

*Ask the LORD to strengthen your love and commitment to your pastor(s) and church, or to lead you to the right one if you don't have one. God can work powerfully online, if there are no local Bible-believing churches in your area yet.* ☺

# Hebrew Terms and More for Worship

1 Rejoice in the Lord, O you [uncompromisingly] righteous [you upright in right standing with God]; for praise is becoming and appropriate for those who are upright [in heart].2 Give thanks to the Lord with the lyre; sing praises to Him with the harp of ten strings. 3 Sing to Him a new song; play skillfully [on the strings] with a loud and joyful sound. 4 For the word of the Lord is right; and all His work is done in faithfulness.—Psalm 33:1-4, AMPC

The LORD accepts all true praise and worship; it must be from the heart, and only He can judge the heart.

Also, there are seven "categories" of praise and worship in the Hebrew language, and to me, they are cool!

About 35 years ago, I learned these from Carman (an amazingly creative and dynamic praise and worship leader and songwriter, who is now in Heaven) and I'm so thankful.

I was actually praising the LORD in many of these ways, before I knew what they were called.

I was singing thanks in the shower and otherwise in private, just because the Holy Spirit, Who is our Helper and much more, reminded me some of the ways God has been so very merciful, faithful, generous, patient, kind, loving, forgiving, and more to me through all my mess and deception!

He has truly been helping me to seek Him, and has continued to teach me His precious ways, turning my darkness into Light. Hallelujah!

Blessed be the LORD, for He is good, and His mercy endures forever (Psalm 106:1)!

Also, when I was 5 or even younger, I was making up songs to the LORD and singing them, while swinging in the back yard. I remember that! So, I was praising the LORD even before I really knew what I was doing. Hallelujah!

Psalm 100—A Psalm of thanksgiving and for the thank offering: **"1 Make a joyful noise to the Lord, all you lands! 2 Serve the Lord with gladness!** <u>Come before His presence with singing!</u> **3 Know (perceive, recognize, and understand with approval) that the Lord is God! It is He Who has made us, not we ourselves [and we are His]! We are His people and the sheep of His pasture.**

**4 Enter into His gates with thanksgiving and a thank offering and into His courts with praise!** <u>Be thankful and say so to Him,</u> <u>bless</u> **and** <u>affectionately praise His name!</u> **5 For the Lord is good; His mercy and loving-kindness are everlasting, His faithfulness and truth endure to all generations.**"—Psalm 100, AMPC (underline emphasis mine)

Father God is such a good, good Daddy—we don't have to do everything "properly" for Him to receive our true adoration, infused with childlike trust in Him! You may want to try some of these, but you don't have to. You can just raise your hands and reach out to Him.

(Most of all, true praise and worship is about worshiping Him in your heart. You can lovingly and thankfully sing to Him in your spirit and soul (mind, will, emotions), and He will hear you!

Also, when we sing out loud, there are many that hear it—you, and the holy angels, and the demons. The holy angels love your praise and worship to God, and the demons hate it. It irritates and even scares them. Ha!)

**TODAH** (TOE-dah) - To praise the LORD when things are the very hardest. (This has come in handy many times in my life, and is probably what we true Believers need more than any other kind!)

**BARUCH** (Bah-RUKE) - To bow to the LORD, and to bless Him.

**YODAH** (Yo-DAH) - To raise the hands to the LORD in worship.

**ZAMAR** (Zah-MAHR) - To praise the LORD on an instrument.

**SHABACH** (Sha-BACH) - To shout in victorious triumph to the LORD.

**HALAL** (Hah-LAHL) - To clap and sing loudly in praise to the LORD.

**TEHILLAH** (Ta-HEEL-ah) - To put all the facets of praise together (including dancing) and praise the LORD in high spirits.

Make sure you don't do these in front of people just to get attention, unless you're in a choreographed group worship dance or something. Of course people will be looking at you then.

However, the purpose is not to get them to think how beautiful or anointed or whatever that you are, but to bring glory to Christ!

Most of these are best done in your private time with the LORD.

Another delightful point is that, when you praise and worship the LORD, the holy angels praise and worship with you!

Also, when other people see you earnestly worshiping and praising the LORD, they are inspired; they are seeing the Holy Spirit in action. He is the One Who gives us the desire to thank, praise, and worship Father God and His Son, King Jesus, and helps us to do so.

I learned several parts of American Sign Language a couple decades ago—solely for the purpose of worshiping the LORD.

That is obviously YODAH in action; the raising of the hands in worship.

I told Him years ago that I never wanted the signing to be a distraction to anyone—for I do it at home, in the car, in the kitchen, wherever; and I cannot not do it at church. It is (once the LORD got my former denominationally-challenged hands up in true, free worship about 25 years ago!) something that just naturally flows out of me. I worship the LORD wherever I am, for He has been SO good to me!

It has been a great blessing to me—and an honor to the LORD!—that numerous people have approached me after a service through the years (in different churches, too, in different cities; not that I've been church-hopping, but that I've attended many services in various places as the LORD has led me.), to express their appreciation that the signing I've done in worship has helped them worship more deeply; appreciate the beauty of the LORD more. Praise God!

That's what it's all about—turning the whole focus to Christ alone, Who is worthy of our praise!

Many of those people, who have asked me to teach them to sign, have been surprised to know that I am not certified in ASL; I only learned the signs I know to purely worship Him. I learned by meticulous study of the books and (then) VCR tapes that I watched decades ago, over and over, till I got the signs learned. Then, it was still a progression, and it always will be.

Let the LORD be magnified, and let us exalt His Name together (Psalm 34:3)!

So, you can do the same, whether it's signing, dancing, playing an instrument, singing, serving, giving, leading, crafting, baking, working; whatever we do, let us do it all to God's glory, as the Word says in I Corinthians 10:31.

*Write down at least one way you can worship the LORD in music, with your voice or your instrument—or both!*

# Guard Your Greatest Treasure

**G**uard your heart with all diligence, for from it flow springs of life.– Prov. 4:23, Berean Standard Bible

*TRUEST TREASURE*

Our hearts are our most treasured possessions, and not just because they pump the blood and keep our brains and bodies going.

Our hearts are the symbol God uses in His Word to represent our spirits. And our spirits are the real us. More importantly, if we have accepted Jesus as our Savior, our hearts hold the most precious treasure of all—His Holy Spirit! So the most important thing we will ever do once we receive Jesus into our heart is to protect that most priceless treasure.

Over 600 verses in the Bible talk about our hearts, and it is our hearts—our spirits—that are the thing about us most important to God. It is not how we look. It is not where we live, or where we go to school, or how many nice things we have.

*GUARD YOUR TREASURE*

Think of something you have—a puppy, a necklace, a toy, a CD—that is your very favorite thing of all the blessings God has given you. Now, would you let someone come in and steal it or tear it up, or even spill dirty oil or mud or something on it? Of course not. You love that thing and you take excellent care of it, so you protect it.

But things can sometimes try to take the place of God in our hearts, which means to become more important to us than Him. That is why

1 John says: (My) little children, guard yourselves from idols. (1 John 5:21)

Nothing is more important to us than Jesus. He is our truest Treasure. So it is extremely important that you guard your heart! But, since your heart—your spirit—is inside you and you can't see it, how do you protect it?

With spiritual armor that is also unseen, of course!

*WEAR YOUR SPIRITUAL ARMOR*

The spiritual armor is found in Ephesians 6:10-18. The different pieces of the armor of God stand for various ways we who are true believers can protect our hearts from the evil plans of the enemy.

The last verse also mentions to pray and keep praying, not only for ourselves but for others, and to watch. To watch means to be on the lookout for evil, just like a good guard does. So to guard your heart is to keep watch to protect it from evil.

One way to guard your heart is to obey those the Lord has put in authority over you.

So, to guard your heart, follow verses 1-3 of the same chapter of Ephesians: Children, obey your parents in the LORD: for this is right. Honor thy father and mother; (which is the first commandment with promise;) That it may be well with thee, and thou mayest live long on the earth. (Eph. 6:1-3)

Other excellent ways to guard your heart are to read and memorize God's Word: to speak God's Word aloud; to pray, especially to pray His Word; to worship Him; and to think on good things.

God actually commands us to do all of these things, for He knows that the most important thing we will ever do once we receive Jesus is to guard our hearts. He will help you. If you feel weak, or like you keep messing up in guarding your heart, just ask Him to help you. He will give you strategies for victory to help you guard your greatest treasure!

*Write at least two ways you can guard your treasure(s).*

# On Being an Heir

The passing of my husband's father (a widower) to Heaven and the processing of his will has given me deeper understanding of what it means to be an heir.

Many parents, in preparation for their passing, prepare a last will and testament where they leave their earthly possessions to their children or heirs. Just as my husband's father wanted to bless his four children (heirs) as equally as possible with the possessions he left behind, so too has God through the death of Jesus made us heirs of all things.

Amazing! Just by believing in Him, He gave us the right to become children (heirs!) of God (John 1:12).

Back to my husband's father's will. The will, carefully prepared in specific detail years earlier, was read by the lawyer in the presence of all the children and their spouses. It listed in detail what each would receive, upon agreement.

The agreement was the key, for each child also had the right to refuse to receive the inheritance.

The lawyer also asked the four children if there were any other children known to have been born to their father and mother. There was no exception; no one other than the heirs were due the benefits of the inheritance.

What God has done for us through the death on the cross of Jesus Christ His Son was not only explain to us in His Word God's last (final, supreme, total) will and testament, the New Covenant that, just by believing in Jesus we become heirs (joint-heirs with Christ), but that all we already have been given by God is listed in His will and testament, the Bible!

However, far too many Christians, including myself, in the past, have been deceived by the enemy into unbelief. We have sometimes not really believed that God means what He says. What a shame and a tremendous loss!

But we can reverse that by simply choosing to believe! Our faith is born in our hearts—our spirits, which is the real us—and must supersede our minds. In other words, we must tell our minds to shut up and speak out of our mouths that we believe God and His Word!

That is what faith is—believing God means what He says!

As I observed the my husband and his three siblings hear the reading of the will, discuss the will, agree with the will, and sign their names to receive the benefits of the will, I was struck with the simplicity of it all. All they had to do to receive the blessing of their father through his will was to believe he meant what he said, and agree to receive it.

All we have to do is believe and receive what God has done for us to receive our inheritance!

There is an enemy who wants to keep us out of it, of course, but we continue to believe and speak out the Word of God—the Covenant—and to thank and praise the Father that His Spirit and His angels and the LORD Jesus Christ are working with us for us to know and apprehend and enjoy all that is ours as heirs of God!

If my husband's father had not wanted his kids to receive any blessing from him, he would have stated that the money and possessions were to go to someone else.

If God had not wanted all who would receive Him through Jesus to become His children to get what Jesus died to share with us (not only eternal life once this earthly life is past, but abundance in every good thing on earth!), then He would not have gone to the tremendous trouble and loss of giving Jesus for us, and resurrecting Him.

If God had wanted to keep our inheritance secret even after sending Jesus, then He would not have had Jesus, the Word in the flesh (John 1:1, John 1:14), preach and teach, and He certainly would not have inspired the 66 books of the Bible, written by various men of God in different countries at different time periods, and had it made into a book so we could read it!

Truly, our Father in Heaven has gone to much effort to make sure that we understand and have access to all He has bequeathed to us—if we will just believe and agree to it!

I was also impressed that, although each heir received several thousand dollars and certain material possessions left to them by their father, that is really nothing compared to what our Heavenly Father has left us through Jesus.

Of course, Jesus was gloriously raised again and lives forever, Hallelujah! He gave Himself that we might live (John 3:16), and enjoy the benefits of being an heir of the living God.

What lavish love the Father has given us! And in His salvation there is every good thing we would ever need or want (John 1:16).

Most precious of all, of course, is the sublime relationship with our dear Father God, our Brother Jesus, the King, and the sweet Holy Spirit Who are One. The LORD is our true wealth and riches.

The living word, the LORD Jesus Christ, is our very life.

So, let us dig deeper into the Word—which is our Daddy God's will that lists exactly what we are due as His beloved heir. May we discover and believe, and thus agree to and acquire and enjoy all that He has given us!

*Ask your Father God to help you share the wonderful Good News about our inheritance in Christ Jesus with people you know!!*

# Our Father God is the Judge

O nce I had to appear before a judge. I was not in trouble, but I needed the judge to make an important decision for me. I was afraid of him, because the people before me had complained and argued and refused to listen—and the judge ordered one of them to jail for 30 days!

When the judge finally motioned to me to approach his high bench, he saw my fear. But he leaned forward, smiled, and whispered, "Yours is a different case."

**[God says] "For I will be leaning toward you with favor and regard for you ..."** Leviticus 26:9, AMPC

I relaxed some, but I knew that this judge, though he was not God, had power to give me what I asked—or throw me in jail if I acted against him. Thank goodness, I knew I had his favor.

There is no judge higher than God. His Word—His Law—is the true Law. But we can't follow His laws unless His Son, Jesus, comes into our hearts. Then God becomes our Father and forgives and favor us. Jesus becomes our Brother and helps us understand, obey, and be greatly blessed by God's Word.

If we don't receive Jesus into our hearts, we are judged and condemned to hell forever when our bodies die. But when we receive Christ Jesus, we are seen as righteous and acceptable to God (II Corinthians 5:21). "Old things have passed away" including our former sinful lives and all things have become new (II Corinthians 5:17).

Have you asked Jesus to be your Savior and Helper today so you can obey Father God and enjoy His favor? He says in Romans 10:13 that all who call upon the Name of the LORD will be saved!

If you want to receive Jesus as your Savior and LORD, say this prayer out loud:

Dear Jesus, I know that without You, I am nothing. I thank You that You died on the cross for the whole world—and You would have done it just for me—to be saved from hell and death and be able to go to live in Heaven with You when our bodies die.

You want to give me Zoe life (John 10:10) now and help me get to know what a wonderful Savior, LORD, and Friend You are! I ask You to please forgive me of all my sins and come into my heart and be my Savior and LORD now. I receive You, and thank You for saving me. In Your Name, amen!

Congratulations! Now that you have received Jesus, there is great rejoicing in Heaven (Luke 15:7), and your name is written in the Lamb's Book of Life (Phil 4:3, Rev.3:5)!

God is forever faithful, and He will always help you—although it may not seem as quickly or the way you thought it would be, but He always hears His children!

*ASK YOUR FATHER GOD to start teaching you how to live for Him. Write at least two ways you think you can do that.*

# Your Words Are Like Apples of Gold

God says many things about words in the Bible and even compares them to apples, as He does in Proverbs 25:11: "Winsome words spoken at just the right time are as appealing as apples gilded in gold and surrounded with silver."

Do you like apples? I do. They are sweet, and good for you. Like all the fruits and vegetables God makes, apples are good to eat to help our bodies stay well.

That is the way our words are supposed to be. Words are very powerful food, and when they are sweet, especially when they are Scriptures from the Word of God, they help us and others stay healthy.

The LORD is the One Who helps us know what to say and what not to say, and how to say it at just the right time. Knowing what His Word says and saying it is one of the very best ways we can be sure that we are speaking sweet words that nourish others, like apples!

People like sweet things, and all of us like to hear words that make us feel good. Ask the LORD to help you speak only good, truthful words to help others know more about how much He loves them!

That doesn't mean that we will never speak anything someone else won't like. The truth is meant to be convicting, and the flesh ("The flesh" is the soulish nature of man—the mind, will, and emotions.) often doesn't like it.

When we speak the Word, it will be sown in the mind of others and start growing. It will either draw them closer to the LORD, or they will try to reject it and turn away.

What happens when you sow the Word is not your responsibility. We plant, we water, and (only) God gives the increase (I Corinthians 3:5-7).

Sometimes, people are hurting so much that they cannot even accept your true compliment or encouragement. Don't take it personally. Deep down, they usually appreciate your effort, even if they don't acknowledge it or respond properly.

Sometimes, just a smile can do wonders, with no words! Also, we can certainly ask the LORD for wisdom to know when to speak and when not to speak, and for just the right thing to say at just the right time, to encourage others—especially in this time of how people all over the world and nation are hurting in so many ways.

What are some sweet words that you can speak to a friend today? Let's pray for the LORD to help us:

Dear Father, Jesus in me is the Living Word, as John 1:1 says. He is also my Wisdom (I Cor. 1:24). I ask that You through Christ Jesus put Your words in my mouth that I may be a blessing to those whom I am around, that they would see and hear Your great love. I receive Your help and thank You for it. In Jesus' Name, amen.

If you have received Christ Jesus as your Savior and LORD, then He hears your prayers, and He will answer!

*Now, ask the LORD to show you opportunities to let Him sow sweet word-seeds through you! It may not be the same day, or even the same week, but He will. You can also ask Him to make you sensitive to His timing and the people who need His words through you.*

# Our Awesome God Still Does Miracles!

Hebrews 13:8 (Berean Standard Bible) says, **"Jesus Christ is the same yesterday and today and forever."**

Our God, the true and only awesome God, never changes! He did miracles thousands of years ago, and He still does them today!

A "miracle" is a mighty work of God that displays His power. The miracles of God overcome every natural law, because God created this world and everything in it.

He is all-powerful (omnipotent), all-knowing (omniscient), and everywhere at once (omnipresent). There is nothing and no one more powerful than Him!

God never does miracles to show off. First, He doesn't need to. He is God!

Second, He does miracles for people because He loves us. He is Love (I John 4:16), and all of His works are motivated by the purest love there is.

Many miracles cannot be seen, because they happen inside people's hearts and minds and bodies. But they are very real. We can't see gravity, but it is very real.

The best miracle is when a person becomes born again—as a new creature in Christ! (2 Cor. 5:17)

God also does miracles we can see, and we will see them more often as the time grows near for King Jesus to return!

What miracles do you know about? Have you been born again?

If you would like to be born again by receiving Christ Jesus as your Savior and LORD so you can have a victorious life on earth, and live with Him forever in Heaven (Paradise) when your body dies, then say this prayer out loud:

LORD Jesus, I thank You for dying on the cross for me, and I ask You to please forgive me of my sins and come into my heart and be my Savior, LORD, and best Friend for life. I renounce all sin, satan, and every evil thing I've said and thought. I thank You for your love and receive you now. I thank You that You will start helping me live the life I've always wanted! in Your Name, amen!

CONGRATULATIONS on making the best decision of your life!

Now, there is a great celebration in Heaven, and Jesus, through His pure blood shed on the cross, has brought you into the Royal Family of God, the great God Jehovah!

*Ask God to help you find the right Bible and friends and church, so you can start studying how to live to enjoy this new life to your best and His glory!*

# Put on Your Armor

Ephesians 6:11 (AMPC) says, **"Put on God's whole armor [the armor of a heavy-armed soldier which God supplies], that you may be able successfully to stand up against [all] the strategies and the deceits of the devil."**

If you have made the ultra-wise decision to ask the LORD Jesus into your heart to be your Savior, then you have joined the Service! You have become a soldier in God's army, and He has given you special armor to wear, called the Armor of Light.

This armor is spiritual, which means you cannot see it. But it is very real!

The different pieces of armor are listed in Ephesians 6:10-18. The armor includes most things soldiers have: a helmet, a belt, a breastplate, special shoes, a shield, and a sword. Verse 18 also mentions prayer, which also gives us protection.

You can put on your armor every day, by quoting these Scriptures. These are mighty words that King Jesus, the Captain of our Salvation, the God of the Angel-Armies, has given us; mighty armor to wear so we can be wise against the enemy's plans and block and stop his every move.

So gear up, soldier, and know that in King Jesus, you have the victory!

Once you receive Christ Jesus as your Savior and LORD, you are given the Armor. Put each piece on—you can say each out loud as you do—and then never take the Armor off.

Each piece of The Armor is necessary and powerful—(1) The Belt of Truth; (2) The Shoes of the Gospel of Peace; (3) the Breastplate of Righteousness; (4) The Helmet of Salvation; (5) The Shield of Faith; (6) The Helmet of Salvation and the Sword of the Spirit, which is the Word of God.

The passage also exhorts us to pray on every occasion in the Spirit.

*Ask the LORD for greater understanding and application of you being a soldier of Light in His army, and of your protection through the Armor of God! He will help you!*

# How to Please God (Part 1 of 3)

Many times, you will hear your parents and your pastors and teachers at church talk about pleasing God. What that means is to trust in God's plan for our lives, and obey Him (Prov. 3:5-6, I Peter 4:1).

God's Plan is always good for us (Jeremiah 29:11). He is Love (I John 4:8) and He is faithful!

**"[They are living memorials] to show that the Lord is upright and faithful to His promises; He is my Rock, and there is no unrighteousness in Him."**— Psalm 92:15

The LORD makes His plan for us simple to understand (2 Cor. 11:3). He wants us to know how to please Him, because He loves us and wants to bless us with a wonderful life in every way (Jer. 29:11)!

The first step is this: To believe that Jesus died on the cross for our sins, and ask Him to forgive and cleanse us, and come in our hearts and be our Savior and LORD (John 3:15-17; Romans 3:23; Romans 6:23; Romans 10:13).

Many people worship many gods, and think Jesus is just "one more god."

NO! Jesus is God, and through faith in His pure blood shed on the cross is the only way any person can truly please God and get into Heaven (John 1:1; John 10: 1, 7, 9; John 3:15-17)!

Just like our parents are pleased with and love us because we are born into their family, God is pleased with us when we are born again through believing in His Son Jesus.

After that, we please the LORD and earn rewards by spending time with Him, trusting and obeying Him, and loving others.

We will talk about these in parts 2 and 3.

*Write down some ways that you already know you please God. He will help you think of them.*

# How to Please God (Part 2 of 3)

In part 1, we determined that the first step to pleasing God is believing in Jesus as our Savior and LORD.

We can please God by showing love, even if we are not born again by believing in Christ Jesus as our Savior and LORD.

When our bodies die (and everyone's will, unless they are alive when King Jesus returns to take with Him to Heaven all who truly believe in Him!), then our spirits and souls (heart and mind/will/emotions) will be eternally, forever, grievously separated from God (Who is Love, and all that is good!), and there will be eternal torment.

No one is eternally separated from God, Who chooses to believe in Him!

He is very merciful and gracious, patient, and long-suffering, not willing that any person whom He created (and He created every one of us and gives us every breath!) should be apart from Him.

He created Adam and Eve and told them to have lots of kids, because He wanted a huge Royal Family, Who could love Him back—forever! Hallelujah!

So, until we choose to realize our need for Christ Jesus, and become born again by agreeing with what Jesus did for us on the cross, we don't have a true relationship with Him, and we can't ever ultimately please Him (John 3:15-17; Romans 3:23; Romans 6:23; Romans 10:13).

God is the God of Family; of Loving, pure Relationship!

God, Who created us all, and loves us so much He sent Jesus His Son to die for us on the cross, so His blood could cover us and wash us clean from our sins (John 3:15-17, Romans 5:6 and 10:13), wants to be our Father!

That can only come when we become friends with His Son, Jesus, and ask Christ Jesus to be our Savior and LORD.

So, it's by believing in God's mercy and grace that gets us to Heaven—never by anything good we do, nor by the wrong we don't do! If God was counting those things for us to be saved, none of us would ever make it!

The LORD loves us all so much, that He makes it very easy to every human in the world, no matter where they are or even if they've done a lot of bad things (and we've all messed up, because every person is born into sin, because of Adam and Eve's treason against God in the Garden of Eden! Romans 3:23 and 6:23).

He has chosen to forgive us all ahead of time—and it's up to us to choose His matchless gift of Salvation!

He even helps us, by His Holy Spirit, to hear about Him (like you're hearing about Him by reading right now!), and want to be part of His eternal Royal Family!

So if you haven't yet asked Jesus to be your Savior and LORD, you can ask Him right now.

Just ask Him out loud to forgive you of your sin. Then say you renounce your sins, satan, and all evil speaking, and ask the LORD Jesus to come into your heart and be your Savior, LORD, and best Friend forever!

At that moment, you will become born again into the Royal Family of God! Your spirit will be regenerated—snatched from the devil and hell—and translated into the glorious victorious Kingdom of Light!

You will please God forever because of your new spiritual status as the Righteousness of God in Christ Jesus!

Once you are born again through your faith in the shed blood of Christ Jesus, the unique and only Son of God, you can start earning rewards by pleasing Him with your good behavior. This is very much like obeying your parents and earning special blessings or an allowance or something—but you have to be born into their family first, because you have to be their children that they love and care for and give you chances to earn rewards.

The more you get to know Jesus, the more you will love Him, for He will become your very best friend. As you do things like pray, read His Word, and worship Him, you will want to do them because you love Him, not just to earn blessings!

He will show you ways to earn blessings and love others so they can know Him too.

*What ways can you think of to bless those you know, and to help them see the LORD, and want to be part of His Family, or draw closer to Him? Helping others with a good heart and attitude brings glory to Father God.*

# How to Please God (Part 3 of 3)

We know that we can never please God until we first ask His Son, Jesus, to forgive us for our wrongs, cleanse us and come into our hearts, and be our Savior and LORD. That is the only way we can get into Heaven when our body dies (John 3:15-17).

But after that, we please God by trusting His Word and obeying Him, and showing respect, just like we trust and obey our parents, teachers, pastors and other people in charge over us.

I Peter 2:13-14 says, 13 **"Submit yourselves for the Lord's sake to every human institution, whether to the king as the supreme authority 14 or to governors as those sent by him to punish those who do wrong and to praise those who do right."**

Sometimes we may not understand why people in charge over us are telling us to do something—or not do something—and we may not like it. We may think we know a better way.

But unless these people are telling us to do something against God's Word, then God expects us to obey. When we obey authority, we please Him.

It is usually okay to very respectfully ask questions or make a comment about an instruction. But we must remember that God put those people in authority over us and that He knows best, and it is His will for us to obey them. When we obey them, we please and honor God.

*Is it easy for you to obey? List three ways you could obey even better (like, "more quickly, more sweetly," etc.)*

# Jesus' Love is the True Power!

We Were Made For Power.

People want power. Magic is a form of power. But according to the Bible, it is wrong.

The LORD Elohim (The Creator of all life and all good) has made us to be spiritual beings, for we all come out of Him, the Holy Spirit!

It is natural for us to be interested in spiritual things, and to exercise power (dominion), which God gave Adam and Eve at the Garden of Eden.

However, when Adam sinned and sold out to the devil, the power and spiritual things were overall perverted.

Now, the only safe and right spiritual things are those that pertain to the goodness of God; that come out of Him, through faith in what the atoning blood of Christ did for us on the cross (John 3:15-17; John 5:6; Romans 3:23, 6:23, and 10:13)!

Otherwise, spiritual things are from the enemy, the deceiver and destroyer, and father of lies.

Dangers of Deception; Being Tricked

There are various forms of "magic," and before I knew how to really honor and LORD Jesus Christ and realize that He wanted to (like every truly loving Father!) keep me away from harm and help me experience only good (which was His Plan from the Beginning, in the Garden of Eden!), I thought it was interesting, and did a little light dabbling.

I was tricked. The deception I was in affected every area of my life, from my creative gifts and energy, to my marriage, and more; even endangering me with a suicidal spirit, where I wanted to end my life!

If something is from God; if He is in it, it will help people—and have *no* sinister (wrong; evil) motives. It will only be to help others because of Love, not to benefit anyone financially or otherwise.

The true God, Who created every person and the universe, and everything good, is forever and only good. His only motive is to help people; to bring them freedom and peace and joy and restoration; protection, abundance; rest and ultimate satisfaction in the deep relationship with Him, Who is Father God to those who choose His Son, Christ Jesus.

I have so regretted and repented of that, and the LORD helped me, in His gracious patience and loving mercy, to turn back to Him, by reading His Word, praying, getting rid of the junk, and leading me to true worship, and programs and churches that truly taught the Bible. Thank goodness!

In these days, there is even more of the wicked "mixture" between darkness (evil) and Light (the Truth of God).

Magic, or witchcraft, takes many forms—"black" (where people openly worship the devil), or "white" (where witches pretend to do good but are still working with the devil).

Magic includes many forms; from mocking and mimicking the power of God (only to a point, just like the wicked magicians in the Bible when Moses confronted the Pharoah to deliver the Israelites from slavery, in Exodus); Darkness; whatever is against God and His Word *is* slavery!) with "white magic" to deeper, blatantly darker "black magic" to all kinds of items and games and art and shows and other stuff.

Magic vs. Miracles

Magic, or false power, is when the magicians that worked for Pharaoh could only imitate the first few miracles God did through

Moses. They couldn't even make the frogs and locusts go away, much less keep their children from being killed.

But miracles happened when God protected His people them from the avenger angel with the covering of the blood of the lamb, parted the ocean for His people to walk through on dry land, and then let it go back to drown the Egyptians as they chased the Hebrews.

In 1 Kings 18, the 450 prophets who worshipped the false God called Baal dressed up and spent all morning doing dumb dances, straining their voices trying to get Baal to wake up (dead gods never wake up), and even cut themselves with knives, hoping their blood and scars would get Baal's attention.

What kind of "god" is it that won't even listen (he can't hear anyway; they just made him up!), and expects you to hurt yourself on purpose?

As one well-known minister says, "Cutting among kids is not new; it goes back thousands of years. It's the same demon that causes it now that caused it then!"

We see a real miracle in 1 Kings 18. Elijah the prophet, who had challenged the prophets of Baal to a contest to prove who was the real God, looked up to Heaven (after the Baal-worshippers had their turn). He said, "Where is the Lord God of Elijah? Lord, show these people that You are God by answering by fire!"

And instantly, the God of Heaven, the true God Who is the true power, sent fire from Heaven and burnt up the sacrifice. Even the water and stones were burned!

The true Power of God comes through the baptism of the Holy Spirit—the true Power of God. When you believe on the LORD Jesus Christ and ask for Him to baptize you in the Holy Spirit, He will!

**"So if you who are evil know how to give good gifts to your children, how much more will your Father in heaven**

**give the Holy Spirit to those who ask Him!"** - Luke 11:13, Berean Standard Bible

God actually commands us to be baptized in the Holy Spirit, in Ephesians 5 **"Do not get drunk on whine, which leads to reckless indiscretion. Instead, be filled with the Spirit."** – Eph. 5:18, Berean Standard Bible

And once you receive this "baptism by fire," He can do miracles through you!

One of the wonderful miracles about being baptized in the Holy Spirit is being able to speak another language—perhaps several other languages!—without ever having to study.

It is actually the Holy Spirit speaking those other languages through us, so that other people, who don't speak English or whatever language you speak, can hear how Jesus died for them and they will realize they need Him as their Savior, so they can go to Heaven and have a wonderful life here on earth!

That happened in the Bible, and it happens today; people hear the miracle of God speaking about Jesus in their own language through people—including kids like you!—and they receive the Lord as their Savior, making Heaven glad and the devil mad!

Just like when I was a young teen, and (wrongly, dangerously) found the things of witchcraft fascinating, they can seem "fun" and "harmless".

They are not!

All of these things are against God!

The LORD knows we want to have fun. We are supposed to have fun—but in a safe, and strengthening way, that helps us grow and does not harm us in any way—nor other people!

God is Holy! True power comes from His love through the LORD Jesus Christ (John 3:16, Romans 5:6)!

Yes, God is holy, and He is also all good. He is Light, and in Him is no darkness at all! Hallelujah!

In this world, it's kind of hard to know what true purity is, because it's been so perverted and distorted; even in the Church!

But God is arising, and moving by His Spirit in this, His earth (Psalm 24:1, 2 Peter 3:5), and starting to expose the darkness more and more, and clean up not only the Church, but all areas of life!

He does that by partnering His power with our earnest prayers for change; for cleansing; for *rightness* with Him!

Just like in the Bible, the enemy comes when he can to plant "tares" (Matthew 13:27-40; weeds of deception and destruction) in the middle

He hates magic, because it's a delusion, deception, distraction, and thus destruction (Lev. 19:26, Jer. 14:14, 2 Tim. 3:9)—and a great dilution of true power, which comes from the LORD God Jehovah, Elohim, alone!

The devil is the father of lies (John 8:44), and he uses magic to keep people away from the true power—Jesus Christ!

(By the way, I don't mean the "magic"—which is really illusion/ sleight-of-hand/tricks that our eyes are not fast enough to see/ distractions—that the magicians on television do. These are methods they have learned to appear to be "magic", and you can learn those tricks too, if you know the secrets and techniques, and practice long enough. ☺ )

The entire Holy Bible is about God and Jesus and the Holy Spirit, Who are One. Revelation 1:8 speaks of Jesus Christ: **"I am the Alpha and the Omega, the Beginning and the End, says the Lord God, He Who is and Who was and Who is to come, the Almighty (the Ruler of all)."**

But when people understand the love of God—through Jesus dying on the cross for us and giving us a wonderful life—they don't want to practice magic anymore!

They turn to God and are saved and delivered, just like the people in the Bible in Acts 19:19 (AMP): "And many of those who had practiced curious, magical arts collected their books and [throwing them, book after book, on the pile] burned them in the sight of everybody."

Many people are deceived, and wrongly believe magic is good. Many people have died or otherwise have suffered harm, because they fooled with the powers of darkness.

But why would they want mere magic and darkness, bondage and fear, when they can have the wonderful love and freedom and true power of Jesus the Christ

If you want to repent of operating against the LORD Jesus Christ, Who is God (John 1:1) and Who shed His pure blood that you could be born again into the true Family of Power—the Family of God—then you can pray this prayer:

"LORD Jesus, please forgive me of all my sins. I renounce sin, satan, magic, and every evil thing and word I've done. Cleanse me with Your pure blood, and please come into my heart by Your Spirit and be my Savior, LORD, and best Friend forever. Take my life and do something wonderful with it. In Your Name, amen!"

CONGRATULATIONS ON THE BEST DECISION YOU'VE EVER MADE! Get ready, for the LORD Jesus will help you get to know Him and start operating in true Power!

Magic is not the power you want. It will only cause you much trouble!

Miracles are mighty manifestations (proof) that God is real, that He lives, that He is the only True Power. God is omnipotent, "all powerful." He is eternal. He is and was and always will be. He is the Champion!

So smart ones like you choose to ask for the baptism of the Holy Spirit, the true Power—of God!

*Now, how can you help your friends and family to know more about the God of Miracles—Jesus Christ, the God of Pure Love!—so they can have the true Power, too?*

# How to Look Like Jesus

**You are to be holy to Me because I, the LORD, am holy, and I have set you apart from the nations to be My own.**—Leviticus 20:26, Berean Standard Bible

God Commands Us to Be Holy

Ever entered or seen a look-alike contest? That is where two people who are not related look so much like each other that hardly anyone can tell them apart! And our goal is to look like Jesus!

We do that by becoming holy—by following all of His ways, by reading and hiding His Word in our heart that we might not sin against Him; by praising Him; and by talking to Him all the time in prayer; and, of course, by not doing what we know is wrong. All of these things help us to look more like Him.

To become holy is a command in the Old Testament, and, just like the Ten Commandments, it is true for today, for every person who has accepted Jesus. He died so He could have many, many little brothers and sisters, or "Christ-like ones," which is what the word, "Christian" means.

What It Means to Be Holy

But to be holy, we first have to understand what it means. The original language of the Old Testament is Hebrew.

So I looked in a Strong's Concordance, which is a big book that has Hebrew and Greek words to help us understand our English Bibles. Strong's says that the use of "holy" in Leviticus 20:26 means "sacred (morally)" and also holy as God, an angel, a saint.

When we believe by faith in Jesus, our spirits become one with Him. We become saints; we are seen as holy by the Lord!

Just as your parents love you and are proud of you just because you are theirs—even when you mess up—how much more God loves us and is proud of us no matter what. They usually see their children as righteous, just like God does, through the blood of His Son, Jesus.

In Webster's Dictionary on the Internet, I found that "holy" comes from the Old English word "whole" and means "one perfect in goodness and righteousness" and "divine."

To truly look like Jesus—to truly become holy in our bodies and minds and keep our spirits right before the LORD—we must become like Jesus. He is perfect in goodness and righteousness. We are not, but as we continue to submit to His Word, He perfects us.

The best way to become holy is to act like Him—in wisdom, purity, faithfulness, gentleness, and love, to name some of His qualities.

The Gospels, which are the books of Matthew, Mark, Luke, and John, show us how He acted when He was on earth. The more we read them, and the entire Bible which is filled with how God is and wants us to be, the more we will understand how to please Him.

<u>Rewards of Being Holy</u>

Our loving Father God loves to reward us for good behavior—even though every single thing we do that's right and good comes from Him to start with! Not only did He give Jesus to save us from death and hell, but He also loves to bless us with special gifts all the time. And the more we look like Jesus by becoming holy, the more pleased He will be

He will just continue to pour out His blessings, like your parents love to bless you! The best part is, the more holy we become, the more useful to Him we are, and the more we look like Him—and the more exciting things we get to do as His representatives.

Thank goodness, God is not "religious" or legalistic. That's where some people get the wrong idea about Him. He is the Spirit of freedom, and gives every person a totally free will.

He also tells us to use our freedom wisely.

Galatians 5:1 (Berean Standard Bible) says, **"It is for freedom that Christ has set us free. Stand firm, then, and do not be encumbered once more by a yoke of slavery."**

2 Timothy 2:21-22 says that, **"21 So if anyone cleanses himself of what is unfit, he will be a vessel for honor: sanctified, useful to the Master, and prepared for every good work. 22 Flee from youthful passions and pursue righteousness, faith, love, and peace, together with those who call on the Lord out of a pure heart."**

*LET'S ASK HIM TO HELP us look more like Him today, by getting rid of those things from our lives that are against Him, and bringing into our lives what pleases Him!*

# Affirming My Students

I don't remember if I told my fourth-graders in the public school that their daily affirmations were based on the Bible. I think it would have been a blessing to most of those sweeties, if they'd known—but it may have created some problems with the administration. (Yeah, probably!)

However, almost every one of my students immediately loved saying the "7 Affirmations" and would compete to lead, day after day. We'd stand, say the "Pledge of Allegiance", then do the Affirmations. They loved it.

My order of operations was that, during the nine weeks, every student would lead the class (even if they didn't want to; I'd let another student with whom they were friends stand with them if needed), usually several times.

Sometimes, a student would try to be funny, and say them too quickly, or in a high-pitched voice. It was a distraction, so when that happened, I'd have them start again. It didn't take long for the other kids to tell the distracting students to "Shut up!" and then we'd start again.

All of these are based on the Word of God!

I believe, because our Father God is so good, so all-knowing, so eager to bless us, that His Spirit overshadowed these words when my students spoke them in unison.

I could see the heart in almost all of my students, every morning, as they said them. A couple were reluctant on some days—but they were still hearing them, and thus, those good seeds were being planted, and watered!

Another thing about the Word of God is that, once it's rooted in the heart, it remains!

During the last few months of the year, my word processing program that worked with the interactive whiteboard was never repaired, even though I requested it. So, I came in one day and could not project the affirmations, as I had been doing for months, for the class to read.

However, a few students jumped up and eagerly volunteered to lead the class from memory!

I was so blessed, and close to tears, as I saw and heard their eager hearts to lead their classmates in those inspiring words, with no writing on the board—*for the affirmations were written in their hearts!* Glory to God!

The LORD is so very faithful! He always puts His blessing on our genuine efforts to help others, even if they don't show appreciation.

After all, He says in His Word that, when we do it to the "least of these," or "the littlest one," that we do it for Him. Praise Him, our good and kind and gracious, merciful, faithful Master Who loves us so much He died for us!

The LORD will give you strategies—including affirmations like these—to help you and your family be stronger and closer to Christ. He will help you, in whatever detailed ways are the right fit for you, your family, your students, and anyone else you want to pray for, speak His Word over, etc.

ON THE NEXT PAGE ARE the affirmations.

*Say them out loud daily, and they can help build your confidence and excellence!*

# 7 Affirmations for Students

These are the Bible-based affirmations that the LORD led me to have my sweet, smart public school students say daily.

*"USING MY POWER OF CHOICE:*

1. I control myself.

2. I show respect to myself and others.

3. I am wise, so I obey my leaders.

4. I am excellent.

5. I am trustworthy.

6. I am quick to help others.

7. I am special and loved, and I believe it."

(They loved it, and memorized them quickly, so that when the electronic whiteboard wouldn't work, they didn't even need it; the affirmations were in their hearts!):

# A Few Ways to Bring Heaven to Earth

"Heaven on earth" is the Presence of God, Who is Love (I John 4:8).

Love, joy, peace, and all the fruit of the Spirit (Galatians 5:22) is what we are created to experience, and the most we experience God, the more we understand and enjoy Him!

Who (what true Believer in Jesus Christ, anyway) does not want a Heavenly life?

The LORD makes it easy (which was always His plan, staring with the Garden of Eden in Genesis 1!) for us to have days of Heaven upon earth—a taste of what it will be like when we are with Him forever in Heaven! Hallelujah!

When the LORD draws us by His Spirit and brings us to saving faith in the LORD Jesus Christ, during which we realize our sin and deep need to be forgiven and cleansed by the blood of Jesus, then we receive Christ Jesus as our Savior and LORD (John 3:14-17).

We are sealed for Heaven by the Holy Spirit, and Christ Jesus—the Essence of Heaven!—comes into our hearts to live with us forever.

**9 He has saved us and called us to a holy calling, not because of our works, but by His own purpose and by the grace He granted us in Christ Jesus before time began. 10 And now He has revealed this grace through the appearing of our Savior, Christ Jesus, who has abolished death and illuminated the way to life and immortality through the gospel.** – II Timothy 1:9-10, Berean Standard Bible

Hallelujah!

**21 Now it is God who establishes both us and you in Christ. He anointed us, 22 placed His seal on us, and put His Spirit in our hearts as a pledge of what is to come.** -II Corinthians 1:21-22, Berean Study Bible

Hallelujah!

Here are three ways that can definitely help you experience more of Heaven on earth:

(1) Read and study, speak, and memorize God's Word.

**18 Fix these words of mine in your hearts and minds; tie them as reminders on your hands and bind them on your foreheads. 19 Teach them to your children, speaking about them when you sit at home and when you walk along the road, when you lie down and when you get up.**

**20 Write them on the doorposts of your houses and on your gates, 21 so that as long as the heavens are above the earth, your days and those of your children may be multiplied in the land that the LORD swore to give your fathers....**—Deuteronomy 11:18-21, Berean Study Bible

(2) Worship the LORD. Ultimately, this means in every area of life—to use the wisdom He gives us (His Word!) to consecrate ourselves to His will and His way—which is, of course, the very best life for us, His kids; which brings honor and blessing and abundance!

**...17 I love those who love me, and those who seek me early shall find me. 18 With me are riches and honor, enduring wealth and righteousness.19 My fruit is better than gold, pure gold, and my harvest surpasses choice silver.**—Proverbs 8:17-18, Berean Standard Bible

He is the God of Heaven and earth (Genesis 1), and our Father Who has adopted us on purpose, to lavish His Love on us for eternity! Hallelujah!

**"O LORD, God of Israel, there is no God like YOu in heaven or on earth, keeping Your covenent of loving devotion with Your**

servants who walk before You with all their hearts.—2 Corinthians 6:14, Berean Standard Bible

23 But a time is coming and has now come when the true worshipers will worship the Father in spirit and in truth, for the Father is seeking such as these to worship Him. 24 God is a Spirit, and His worshipers must worship Him in spirit and in truth. – John 4:23-24, Berean Standard Bible

4 But when the time had fully come, God sent His Son, born of a woman, born under the law, 5 to redeem those under the law, that we might receive our adoption as sons. 6 And because you are sons, God sent the Spirit of His Son into our hearts, crying out, "Abba, Father!". Galatians 4:4-6, Berean Standard Bible

<u>(3) Praise Him and be thankful for all of His goodness—all the days of your life!</u>

The LORD deserves and honors our appreciation of Him! He alone is worthy of the highest praise! Also, of course, it's a win-win; when we praise the LORD, our minds are set on Him and positives, and we feel better—which is part of Heaven on earth!

4 Enter His gates with thanksgiving and His courts with praise; give thanks to Him and bless His name. 5 For the LORD is good, and His loving devotion endures forever; His faithfulness continues to all generations.—Psalm 100:4-5, Berean Standard Bible

17 Pray without ceasing. 18 Give thanks in every circumstance, for this is God's will for you in Christ Jesus. 19 Do not extinguish the Spirit.—I Thessalonians 5:17-19, Berean Standard Bible

*LIST AT LEAST TWO MORE ways you can enjoy more of Heaven on earth from now on—and teach others how!*

# Have You Seen the Ghost?

Ghosts have been around for centuries, and some people think they're cool. Some people are scared of them. Some people think that ghosts live with them.

But trust me— those ghosts are fakes. And they aren't really nice; they just act that way at first. (It's a trick!) They are demons; disembodied spirits, and no matter how "cute" they may seem at first, their true intent is to do you harm.

The Ghost I'm talking about is the real thing. He's truly friendly and nice. You truly can interact with Him in amazing ways, and He's *the coolest.*

If you don't have The Ghost, then you need Him!! He'll hang out with you everywhere, but He won't bug you. He just wants to be with you, and help you. He is actually very loving, very kind.

There is no other Ghost like Him. He's called The Holy Ghost, or the Holy Spirit. He is the Spirit of Jesus (Philippians 1:9) Who comes to save us from hell and live in our hearts when we cry out to Him for real (Romans 10:13).

He is the eternal God Who wants to take your messed up life and give you a wonderful one (John 10:10)

No other ghost can do that—only the Holy Ghost, the true and eternal Son of God, Who died so you can be free, and have a life better than you can imagine!

Jesus, Who is the Holy Ghost, the Spirit of God, rose again and lives forever to help you! He comes to live in you when you receive Him as Savior, and He desires to fill you to over flowing with His Spirit, to empower you to fully live your destiny and have grace to reach others for Him. (Acts 1:4-7 and Acts 2)

The Holy Ghost wrote the whole Bible (2 Timothy 3:16)!

As Jesus He came to earth to live and die and pay for our wrongs we should have had to pay for, but couldn't. When Jesus the Man ascended back into Heaven, He sent His Spirit as the Holy Ghost—the Holy Spirit—so He could be inside each of us forever, and greatly multiply His Word and His ways.

As the Man Jesus, He was perfect, but still limited, because He was in a human body. But His Spirit (also called "The Comforter") is in our hearts and we don't have to wait in line to speak to Him, like people used to have to do when Jesus was on earth.

When you become friends with Jesus, the Holy Ghost, you get to get into Heaven with God—for free! Want to have The Ghost as your Best Friend and Savior today?

Just say this prayer, and ask God to help you mean it in your heart, then tell people!

<u>Dear Jesus Who is the Holy Ghost, the Spirit of God, I need You. I need You to forgive me of all I've done wrong and cleanse me by Your blood that spilled out on the cross so that I can go free, and become Your friend and go to Heaven to live with You and God.</u>

<u>Please fill me to overflowing with your precious Spirit. Help me to stop letting any other bad ghost hang around! And help me to get to know You while I'm on earth, and share You with others. I thank You for saving and loving and filling me. I love You, Holy Ghost!</u>

*What did you feel or think of when you read this article, and/or said this prayer? Tell the LORD you love Him and are glad He loves you forever!*

# How to Walk in the Will of God

Many times, you will hear your parents and your pastors and teachers at church talk about "walking in the will of God."

What that means is to trust in God's plan for our lives, and obey Him. It sounds simple, doesn't it, kind of like two plus two equals four.

Most of the time, it is simple, unless we try to make it hard. There are many ways to discover and walk in the will of God. The main way is to study the Bible and follow it. It is God's Guidebook for Successful Living.

Sometimes the Bible does not give us specific direction, such as whom to marry or what car to buy, or whom to have as a close friend. But the Holy Spirit Who is God leads us by peace in our hearts. If the peace leaves and does not come back—or is missing to start with—then the LORD is usually warning us away from something or someone.

One of the easiest ways we walk in the will of God is to trust and obey those people He puts over us, such as our parents, teachers at church and school, and other leaders—unless they are telling us to do something against God.

This is another reason we must know what the Bible says, so we'll know the difference between right and wrong. Sometimes we may not understand why they are telling us to do something, or not do something, and we may not even like it. We may think we know a better way.

It is usually okay to very respectfully tell our parents and other leaders what we think about something, and to ask questions. But we must remember that God put those people in authority over us and that He knows best, and it is His will for us to obey them. This is called submitting to authority.

**1 Children, obey your parents in the Lord, for this is right. 2 HONOR YOUR FATHER AND MOTHER (which is the first commandment with a promise), 3 SO THAT IT MAY BE WELL WITH YOU, AND THAT YOU MAY LIVE LONG ON THE EARTH.** – Eph. 6:1-3, Berean Standard Bible

Submitting to authority will continue all your life, no matter how old you are. It is the excellent plan of God, for we all must submit to authority.

Even Jesus submitted to the authority of God the Father. He never did anything other than what God told Him to do, and He never said anything other than what God told Him to say.

**28 Jesus said, "When you lift up the Son of Man, then you will know that I am *He,* and I do nothing on My own initiative, but I speak these things as the Father taught Me. 29 "And He who sent Me is with Me; He has not left Me alone, for I always do the things that are pleasing to Him."** - John 8:28-29

Most important, Jesus submitted to the authority of God when He agreed to go to the cross and die to pay for the sins of every person that would ever be born. Jesus did not want to go to be beaten and made fun of and spit on and killed, especially since He had never done anything wrong!

He even very respectfully asked God the Father if there was some other way to save all people from the horrible death of hell because of their sins.

But God said no. So Jesus walked in the will of God by submitting to the authority of the Father; He went to the cross and died for our sins, so we don't have to. Hallelujah!

Then God gloriously rewarded Him, for there is always a reward for walking in the will of God by submitting to authority. Some of the rewards Jesus received were that He came back to life and will never die, seized again the leadership of the universe from the devil our enemy, and lives forever as the awesome and perfect King of kings.

But His best reward is that He became the Savior; He provided a way for every person in the world who will believe and accept that He died for them and rose again, to know Him and come live with Him forever in Heaven! So it was definitely worth the LORD Jesus walking in the will of God by submitting to the Father's authority.

Thank goodness He did, or none of us could be saved!

We all like rewards, and walking in the will of God by submitting to authority will bring us blessings better than we can dream.

The very best reward of all is that our best Friend Jesus gives us the happiest life on earth and a glorious life in Heaven with Him when we walk in God's will!

*What are at least two ways that you know you are walking in God's will daily?*

# How to Choose the Best Bible for You

When I heard Dr. Brian Simmons, the translator of *The Passion Translation Bible®* speak in Texas in the summer of 2019, he shared how he answered a question about to know which the best Bible is.

Quoting himself, he said he answered, "The best Bible is the Bible you *live!*"

I agree, and I speak from experience when I say the LORD can use any version of His Word to help you know Him and His will for your life!

When I was 7, I received a Bible from the church I was going to, because I had participated in the class Scripture memorization lessons and earned the right amount of stars.

Of course, the point of awarding the stars was to encourage us to learn the Scriptures, to hide them in our hearts to help us know how to live the victorious Christian life!

But I was awarded a *King James Bible*. That had some big hard words and expressions in it, especially for a 7-year-old.

However, I was eager to get to know God, and I started reading! I certainly did not understand all I read, but the Spirit of God was working to help me understand what I needed.

I took my Bible to church with me, and the summer when I was 9, listening to the worship music during Vacation Bible School, the light shined in my heart and I knew I needed Jesus to be my Savior.

So I went down and told the preacher that I had believed in my heart that I needed Him and wanted Him to help me be born again, to live with Him in Heaven after my body died, and to get to know Him down here.

So I believed in my heart and spoke it with my mouth, and I was born again (Romans 10:8-10).

That proved that, even though I had only been 7 when I truly started reading the Bible, and even thought it was hard for a 7-year-old to understand such big words, the Word of God is spiritually understood, because a spirit (God) wrote it, and it is our spirit (the real us, the inner core of us; the part that will live forever after our body dies) that understands the Bible.

(That is another reason that any person who is not truly born again can read the Bible a hundred times or more, and never truly understand it. We must have God, the Spirit of Truth, to correctly interpret it for us.)

I used that Bible for years, and would especially cling to it when I was afraid. I still have it in my keepsakes—worn and yellowed white cover and all. I read the KJV exclusively for the next 15 years or so, taking comfort and understanding from it many times.

Then I was told by a pastor of the church I had attended at the time to buy a *Thompson Chain Reference* study Bible. It was also a KJV. The study references and notes helped my understanding go deeper.

A few years later, a friend gave me a New International Version, and it opened up a whole new world of understanding, because it was written in "plain English." So I that strengthened my spiritual walk with deeper understanding.

The last several years, I have very much enjoyed reading my parallel *KJV/Amplified Bible*. I like the way the *Amplified Bible* (also a very close translation from the Hebrew and Greek texts) puts additional definitions in parenthesis to complete the thoughts, thus "amplifying" our understanding.

My husband has read from the *New American Standard Bible*\*, which is even a closer translation from the original Hebrew (Old Testament) and Greek (New Testament) than the *KJV* as well as from the *ESV* (English Standard Version).

He also has a really cool *Greek-Hebrew Keyword Bible*\*, which has the keywords in the *KJV* text marked to correspond to the concordances in the back. It's like having a mini Strong's concordance and *KJV* Bible rolled into one. Very convenient.

I also have a copy of the *Message Bible*\* (translated by Pastor Eugene Peterson). It is extremely easy to read and understand, and very contemporary. Reads almost like a novel.

And, as I told my daughter, when she was almost 12, the Bible has "everything in it you can find on TV," both virtue and vice, but portrayed in the way it should be: against the absolute of the Word of God!

There are many other versions available, of course.

BibleGateway.com[1], or BibleHub.org, or BlueLetterBible.org, or many Bible apps available now.

Also, your local Christian bookstore are excellent places to research the differences of the versions.

There are also many versions available in multiple languages. The LORD Who created every person wants every person to be part of His Royal Family, and He continues to help people translate His Word into the languages of the world!

Until I worked in a Christian bookstore, I had no idea of all the versions of the Word that are available. Many customers were somewhat confused when trying to choose a Bible, so here are tips we want to help you decide which Bible is right for you.

Maybe you've never bought a Bible before, or maybe this is your 20th and you just want to enhance your study with a different version.

---

1.     http://Www.BibleGateway.com

My husband and I have several versions of the Word in our house, you can easily explore multiple versions (including in many other languages!) of the Bible free, online at www.BibleGateway.com, BlueLetterBible.org, BibleHub.org, and more.

That way, you could see which version ministers the most to you before you purchased a hard copy.

We truly live in such a blessed age, to have free 24/7 access to the richness of God's unchanging, infallible, all-powerful Word that is relevant to every age and century!

If you are still not sure, after doing these options, which is right for you, ask your pastor or another true Believer to recommend one that has worked for them.

But the very best advice is to ask Your Father, Who lives inside you from the moment you are born again through faith in the shed blood of Jesus Christ, to lead you to the right one. You may look at several, but He leads us by peace.

When you find the right one for you, you'll know it. You'll most likely have joy and a settled peace about it. The LORD your Daddy God created you and He knows exactly which version you will like the most!

What is the best Bible? According to Dr. Brian Simmons, the translator of The Passion Translation Bible, "The best Bible is the one that you read!"

He can use anything available to teach us more about Himself, His love and provision for us, and how we can be more successful in life!

*Ask the LORD to show you which Bible is best for you. He leads you usually by peace and desire. So, if you are drawn to a certain version, go with that one!*

# Be Like the Moses Sole Fish!

There is a little fish that sharks like to eat, but this little fish—called The Moses Sole Fish—cannot be eaten: simply lies still and secretes a poison, which locks the shark's jaws!

So is our praise and thanksgiving the poison that freezes—and routs—the enemy!

**21 Then Jehoshaphat consulted with the people and appointed those who would sing to the LORD and praise the splendor of His holiness. <u>As they went out before the army, they were singing: "Give thanks to the LORD, for His loving devotion endures forever." 22 The moment they began their shouts and praises, the LORD set ambushes</u> against the men of Ammon, Moab, and Mount Seir who had come against Judah, and they were defeated."** – 2 Chronicles 20:21-22, Berean Standard Bible (underline emphasis mine)

The singers and praisers and worshipers of the LORD God Almighty went out in front of the armed soldiers—and the LORD caused the enemy armies to be confused and fight and destroy each other, instead of God's people!

Jesus Christ is the Same yesterday, today, and forever (Hebrews 13:8), and so when we praise and thank and worship the LORD in the middle of trouble, Daddy God gets involved, and causes the enemy to run away from us and stop his mess!

Hallelujah!

The words of our mouth are very powerful, and the more we can say what we want, and not say what we don't, the better our lives will be. We are created to be "speaking spirits."

I have messed up horribly with my words through the years, and I'm so glad the LORD has been teaching me to repent of those wrong words, and listen to and watch positive things—especially His Word and ways—and stop being around people who talk and act against His Word!

My life has become SO MUCH BETTER since I've been doing that!

Yours will too!

So, if the enemy attacks, you can greatly lessen and shorten—and even stop—his attacks, when other spiritual rules are being followed, by turning your attention to God with praise and worship and thanksgiving. The enemy is jealous and will not hang around to hear us praise God! Hallelujah!

OUR GOD REIGNS and if GOD is for us (and HE IS!), then none can be against us!

As Romans 8:31 says (AMPC), **"What then shall we say to [all] this? If God is for us, who [can be] against us? [Who can be our foe, if God is on our side?]"**

Speaking the Word of God, going to a Bible-believing church regularly, thanking the LORD, praying the Word, and in the Spirit, repenting (making changes as the LORD shows you to), and praising and worshiping the LORD will give you victory—and a better life than you ever could have imagined (John 10:10)!

*Ask the LORD to help you find more Scripture(s) to praise and worship Him today. Write them out, say them, memorize them, and share them!*

# About Communion and How to Take It

The cup of blessing [of wine at the Lord's Supper] upon which we ask [God's] blessing, does it not mean [that in drinking it] we participate in and share a fellowship (a communion) in the blood of Christ (the Messiah)? The bread which we break, does it not mean [that in eating it] we participate in and share a fellowship (a communion) in the body of Christ? — I Cor. 10:16, AMPC

Taking Communion means stopping our busy lives to purposely remember the victorious death of Christ Jesus for us on the cross, where His blood washed away the effects of all our sin!

You can take Communion daily, in your home! Here's how:

1. Get a cracker or tiny piece of bread; one to represent you, and another to represent anyone else for whom you want to pray. The bread or cracker represents the body of Jesus, broken for us that we may be healed (I Peter 2:24, Isaiah 53:5).
2. Get a small cup or glass and put a bit of juice or water in it. This represents the blood of the Lamb, Jesus Christ, shed for us on the cross that we might be born again (John 3:15-17).
3. Find a quiet place where you can focus on the LORD for a few minutes. Start thanking the LORD out loud for His goodness to you; for dying for you and drawing you to Himself, that you might be saved. Sing if you like. Pray in the Spirit; whatever He leads you to do.
4. Lift up the bread to Him—for that is the pattern in the Word, where He took the bread first with His disciples at the

Last Supper (the night before He was crucified), and told them to break and eat it, for it represented His body. Thank Him for allowing His body to be broken, that you and your loved ones might be healed.

5. Eat the bread or cracker thoughtfully, worshipfully.
6. Take the glass with the juice or water and lift it up to Him. This represents His blood shed for the remission of sins. Hallelujah! Before you drink it, thank Him that His blood continuously (never-ending) covers you and makes you acceptable to the holy Father God; washing you forever. Hallelujah!
7. Tell Him He is your victory; your healing; your deliverance; your prosperity; your abundant life (John 10:10); your everything!
8. Drink the juice/water and ask Him to help you take Communion as often as He wants.

He will. When we remember the LORD's death till He returns, we honor Him.

*As one who believes in Christ Jesus, you can take Communion daily at home, and teach other Believers to do the same!*

# A Different Kind of Worship

H ebrews 13:15 (Berean Standard Bible) says: **"Through Jesus, therefore, let us continually offer to God a sacrifice of praise, the fruit of lips that confess His name."**

This is what we think of usually, along with singing and playing a musical instrument, as "worship"—and when done from the heart to bless the LORD, they truly are worship.

Otherwise, I believe that too many of us have strained trying to figure out exactly what "worship" means in addition to the musical type.

When I read this Scripture, verse 16 of Hebrews 13, I rejoiced, and realized that the LORD is so gracious that He sees many things as worship, when they are done to honor Him: **"And do not neglect to do good and to share with others, for with such sacrifices God is pleased."**

So, according to this Scripture, the LORD sees good deeds and being generous with others as "worship"! Hallelujah!

Look what else I discovered, in the verse after that: **17 "<u>Obey your leaders and submit to them</u>, for they watch over your souls as those who must give an account. To this end, allow them to lead with joy and not with grief, for that would be of no advantage to you."**

Wow, obedience is also "worship". That makes sense, for it agrees with what King Jesus said in John 15:14 (Berean Standard Bible) in **14 You are My friends if you do what I command you.**

The LORD is showing us clearly that, while He delights in our worship of Him in music and other ways, He also considers doing good deeds and sharing, along with obeying our leaders (with a good attitude, of course!) a form of worship!

Our God is such a good God! He tells us clearly what He expects from us in His Word, and He gives us the marvelous Holy Spirit—the Spirit of Jesus—to help us and guide us every day and night, 24 hours long.

Sometimes, we have to be quiet and actually ask Him and listen for His reply, for He is a Gentleman! We can also perceive His direction as we praise and worship, and during prayer.

Then we ask Him to help us act on what He says. His commands are not harsh, for His yoke is easy and His burden is light!

So, we can worship the LORD today by doing a good deed.

It won't get you into Heaven—for only your faith in the death of Jesus Christ on the cross for your sins and His resurrection after three days from the dead can do that (John 3:15-17; Romans 3:23; Romans 6:23; Romans 10:13)—but it will bring praise and glory to God in Heaven Who is good all the time, and Who is so worthy of our praise!

You'll feel great! The LORD says that it is "more blessed to give than receive" (Acts 20:35)—because we were created in the image of God, and He is the ultimate Giver!

*Write at least three things you can start doing this week to have fun giving, helping, obeying—worshipping—the LORD God today!*

# Altered Reality (Virtual Reality)

At the mall, my (then) preteen daughter wanted me to participate in a virtual reality ride with her. We chose one of the very few that didn't appear to have demonic or violent or sexual scenes and titles, and that left us with a "runaway ice train" type thing, somewhere in the frozen tundra of Siberia, I suppose.

We leaned back, held the bars, and watched a very large screen that occupied most of our vision. While there were moments I seemed to feel involved in adventure, I still wasn't scared—'cause *I knew it wasn't real*. It was not reality.

In my real world, I could hear people talking, see them walk past and watch me in the game, and, even though it seemed in the game like I was going to smash into stuff and things were falling all around me, barely missing me and the train I was in was running off the tracks, etc., I knew it wouldn't really happen.

I could feel the vibrations and the turning, from my seat, which was moving with the movie, but no matter how things *seemed*, they would not last, for they were not real.

So, during that interesting two minutes, I realized this world we live in is the same—temporary, and not real—compared to the spirit world and eternity.

As 2 Corinthians 4:18 says, **"So we fix our eyes not on what is seen, but on what is unseen. For what is seen is temporary, but what is unseen is eternal."**

Remember, as one pastor has stated, "Everything on earth is temporary. Just keep holding on and believing God, and things will change!" God is our Rock Who never changes, "Jesus Christ the same yesterday, today, and forever." Hebrews 13:8

You can depend on Him, and you'll never regret it!!!

*Ask the LORD to open your eyes to how very temporary this world you live in is; how real the spirit world is, and to help you invest in eternity much more than temporary stuff.*

# Communion Means Remembering Christ on the Cross

"Communion" means many things; closeness, or "intimacy," where you know someone very well and you share secrets. It can also mean celebrating together, by eating together.

According to one pastor, the word for "Communion" is related to thanksgiving, so that when we thank the LORD it is a form of Communion.

All of these things are part of the holy ceremony of Communion.

Although when Jesus held the Last Supper, which we call Communion, or the Eucharist, the eve before His dying on the cross, He was both happy and sad.

Jesus said in Luke 22:15 to the disciples, "...With desire I have desired to eat this Passover with you before I suffer."

**"And He took bread, gave thanks and broke it, and gave it to them, saying, 'This is My body, given for you; do this in remembrance of Me.'"** - Luke 22:19

As believers, most of us have experienced eating the wafer symbolizing Jesus' precious body broken for our healing, and grape juice symbolizing His glorious blood spilled for the forgiveness and cleansing of our sins.

But did you know you don't have to wait until you go to church to take Communion?

As kings and priests and children of the living God, we are free to take Communion in our home! Communion, the breaking of bread with one another, is sharing times and events, and talking about things very important to us; things we wouldn't talk about with just anyone.

And so does He, the risen Lord, desire to "break bread"— to communicate with, talk—with us, and not just at church. Praise the Lord, we are the Church! And He wants to enjoy the intimacy of close relationship with us, His brothers and sisters, wherever we are.

There are many ways to take Communion. Ask the LORD to show you how He wants to do it. The most important thing is to honor God by remembering His death on the cross, and to ask Him to cleanse your heart of sins and wrong thinking.

The main reason we take Communion with the wafers and juice is to represent His body broken for us, and His blood spilled for us; to remember the awesome love Jesus showed for us on the cross.

So when you keep remembering how good the Lord is to you and thank Him in your hearts and out loud, that will bless Him, and He is worthy!

*Ask your parents if you can please take Communion as a family. If they don't want to yet, keep praying. God will open the door and change their hearts, in His time.*

# Are Your Prayers Powerful?

I f you want to make sure your prayers are powerful, do following:
<u>You must receive the LORD Jesus Christ into your heart.</u> Once you believe by faith that He died on the cross for your sins and rose again after three days and now lives forever, and ask Him to forgive you and be your Savior and LORD, He will live inside your heart and help you to live the victorious Christian life.

You won't have to struggle through life by yourself anymore (John 3:15-17; Romans 10:13; Proverbs 18:24; John 15:15)!

Best of all, God the Father will hear your prayers from that moment on (unless you for some reason are scorning Him and have decided to stop believing) because once you receive Jesus into your heart, God will no longer be angry with your sin.

Jesus will have paid the price, and God will see you from that moment on as a new person—the brother or sister of Jesus!

And He will love you just as much!

So, to even get God to hear your prayers, you must become close friends with His Son, Jesus!

(The only prayer God will hear from someone who doesn't know His Son, is the prayer of "LORD Jesus, please forgive my sins and come into my heart to be my Savior and LORD!" (Romans 3:23; Romans 6:23; Romans 10:13))

<u>Go through the Bible and find prayers that are already written out, such as (in no particular order):</u>
Nehemiah 1:5-11
Micah 7:18-20

Ephesians 1:16-21 and 3:14-23
Colossians 1:9-12
Jeremiah 33:3
Hosea 10:12
Zechariah 10:12
Isaiah 45:11 and 43:26
Malachi 3:10-12
I Thessalonians 3:11, 12

These are just a few. You can also find many books with various prayers written out, all based on Scripture.

Pray these out loud and you'll soon connect more than ever with your loving Father!

Pray God's Word back to Him from singular verses. There is great power in praying the Word of God aloud, back to Him! He loves it, and besides touching His heart when you do so, you are getting more of His Word into you, thus strengthening your faith!

You can take most verses of the Bible and make them personal.

It helps me to use an easy-to-understand version of the Bible, such as the *Amplified Classic*, or *The Passion Translation*, although God of course understands every version, and every language on earth. His Spirit will breathe life and understanding for you into whatever version you read and truly seek Him in. He is so very good!

Ask the LORD to show you which verses to pray, and make them personal to you—for the Bible is your guidebook, written to you, from your Father God!

Find those that touch on the things you want to pray about. For instance, if you want to pray about your job or business finances, pray verses such as Proverbs 11:18b: "Thank You, LORD, as Your Word says, "**18The wicked man earns deceitful wages, but he who sows righteousness (moral and spiritual rectitude in every area and relation) shall have a sure reward [permanent and satisfying]."**

You could also use this Scripture about your work: **"Let the loveliness of the LORD our God rest on us, affirming the work that we do. Oh yes. Affirm the work that we do!"** Psalm 90:17

When I bless my loved ones by speaking the Word over them daily, I have often used Psalm 20, parts of verses 4 and 5:" **⁴May He grant you according to your heart's desire and fulfill all your plans. ⁵We will [shout in] triumph at your salvation *and* victory, and in the name of our God we will set up our banners. May the Lord fulfill all your petitions."** – Berean Standard Bible

It is easy and delightful to search the Word of God for treasures of Scriptures that you can quickly turn into personal prayers for you and your loved ones!

Just open the Bible or go to your favorite book, and the LORD will show you many more verses than you have time to pray. But start, and you'll soon be adding verses, memorizing them, and finding that you hear the sweet Holy Spirit speaking them to you just when you need them most.

Enjoy, and remember—your prayers don't have to be long. Sometimes at various hard times in my life, I have literally just said, "Help me, Jesus!" out loud, and He does!

For when we receive Jesus as our Savior and LORD and best Friend, He also becomes our Big Brother forever. Jehovah becomes our Father, and so of course every good brother and father hear and answer the cry of their family member when they call for help!

Hallelujah!

*Ask the LORD to help you also and He will help you memorize more verses that you can arrange into your own personal* prayers!

# What Does Worship Mean to You?

Worship. What does it mean to you? Music? Prayer? Raising your hands? Perhaps an act of service such as giving to the needy? Doing what you know is right—even when you don't feel like it?

Years ago, my little girl and I were getting ready in the bathroom. She watched me as I put on my makeup, and said, "Mama, you can barely see yourself in the mirror for all those notes!" I smiled. Indeed, the mirror was bordered with notecards on which I'd written favorite verses.

The Bible says the Word is like a mirror; it shows the real me, lovely or not. Every morning, I say these verses out loud. Not only does that help me get awake physically, but spiritually as well.

For instance, I have Psalm 25 (Amplified Classic version) printed out and taped to my mirror, and Psalm 20 as well. These Psalms are very comforting and inspiring to me, and I read them out loud almost daily.

All of the precious and powerful promises of the LORD are for every true believer and follower, and speaking them aloud sets my mind on Jesus first thing every morning. To me, that is a form of worship.

True worship can involve these things and more. But most important is the condition of the heart. Worship actually means, in essence, Baruch or Barak - the Hebrew word meaning "to bow down."

This is much more than the physical bowing of the body. It means the bowing—the submission of—the mind, the emotions, the will—to the Lord, and whatever He asks you to do.

Easier said than done. We serve a good, good, God, a truly caring, personal Father Who gives us nothing but unconditional love and endless mercy, and Who is forever faithful, in spite of us.

Still, it has sometimes been much more convenient for me to bow to the Lord while worshipping to music than to obey when I know He is leading me.

The human will is stubborn, and the flesh wants control. It does not like being told by God or anyone else what to do.

Our "flesh" is the carnal part of us that is not our spirit and will never be born again or transformed by the Word, although we control it (our animal-like impulses and desires, even if it's just eating too much) with our spirits and sanctified (washed by the Word of God) minds.

"Will in me to do Your good will," and "Let Your will be done, Lord," and "Make me willing to be made willing," are often my daily prayers, and sometimes several times a day! Other times, when the struggle is particularly strong, I'll pray in the Spirit and say—sometimes shouting!—"Help, Daddy, I can't do this without You!"

And sometimes, worship is simply sitting in the presence of God until He speaks—then acting on what He says.

He knows. He cares. He answers. He hears our cries and helps us to submit to His perfect will. And He alone is worthy of our worship, of our bowing down, of our submitting to what He asks.

He, like a splendid, majestic golden eagle looking down upon the world, sees the big picture. He sees from beginning to end, where we land dwellers can only see what is right in front of our faces.

So we trust Him, God, Who is our Leader, our Father Who has only the best for us, His precious children. So we worship. We bow down to the King, and obey.

*Ask the LORD to help you understand and enjoy worshiping Him even more. He will!*

# God Invented Families!

The family is God's idea! Even before governments were set up in the earth, God established the family, first through Adam and Eve, one man and one woman, as a complete covering for the children, in the Garden of Eden.

God's ideas are always best and there are many wonderful reasons families are an excellent idea.

<u>Loving Families Tell the World about God</u>

One of them is that, by obeying our parents and loving each other, we show the world the greatness of God.

By this we know that we love the children of God, when we love God, and keep his commandments. (1 John 5:2)

He is loving and giving, and puts us in families so we can understand more about how much He loves us. By loving each other, and all people, we show God's love for one another, and people who aren't even in our families.

We also show love for one another when we love God and obey His commandments.

<u>We Have Family throughout the World</u>

Your family may be big or small or medium. No family is the same, and God put you on earth to enjoy having a family, and to help Him have a bigger one!

See, when we tell people how Jesus died for them and they believe in Him (get saved), then they are adopted into God's family. And that is the very best place to be!

Did you know that, if someone believes in Jesus, even if they are from a different country, that they become part of the family of God?

As the Word says in Acts 10:34, "Then Peter began to speak to them: "I truly understand that God shows no partiality, but in every nation anyone who fears him and does what is right is acceptable to him."

That's right, it doesn't matter where someone is from, if they love and believe in what Jesus did on the cross for them, they are your brothers and sisters in Christ, and you are theirs! All believers in Jesus are one big family!

Isn't that wonderful? So, if you know Jesus, you have brothers and sisters all over the world!

The family is where we understand much about how God loves us because we are shown love by our mother and father and brothers and sisters. And we show them love. When we show love to each other, we are showing how God feels about us.

<u>To Love is to Obey</u>

One way we show love and respect to our parents is by following their rules and being respectful while we do it. Obeying our parents is one of God's commands for us. So obeying our parents is one of the ways we show love for Jesus.

**Children, obey your parents in everything, for this is pleasing to the Lord.** - Col. 3:20, Berean Standard Bible

<u>The Defeated Enemy is Trying to Hurt Our Families!</u>

The enemy hates families and tries to make us not obey our parents, and also tries to make brothers and sisters mad at each other so they won't want to be families anymore.

Sadly, the devil has made many people very angry at each other and has succeeded in destroying many families, and that has caused a lot of hurt to this whole world.

But you and I are not going to let him split our families up, are we?! No!

*Write at least two ways you can love your family more.*

# More Ways to Show Love to Our Families

When we know Jesus, we have power in prayer to stop the enemy's work against our families. Even if the rest of our family is not saved, we keep on praying and know that the Lord God hears our prayers, for we are praying in His perfect will!

See, He invented families and He wants them to stay together even more than we do!

Praying is one of the best ways to show love to our families—even if they don't know we pray for them! God sees and hears every prayer.

And, we can show our love for our families by saying sweet things to them, hugging them, telling them, "Thank you for being so wonderful," smiling at them a lot, bragging on them to others, baking cookies for them (with Mom or Dad's or big sister's help), drawing them pretty pictures and writing them love notes or poems.

Your family is a precious gift from God, and we say, "Thank You, Jesus, for our families! Help us to show them more love today!"

*Now, write at least three ways you have been showing love to your family, and also thank the LORD for them!*

# The Glory of God is All Around You

Some people think that the Glory of God is when they see blue smoke, or when people get so overwhelmed with the presence of God that their bodies can't stand it and they fall to the floor, or when people shout or dance or something. And when God truly inspires those things, they do reflect His glory.

However, the true Glory of God is the Spirit of God. When the Spirit of God manifests, which means "shows up," or "appears" or "becomes more concentrated," then miracles occur.

Miracles—things that only GOD can do—are happening around you every day. Miracles are part of the Glory of God.

Some miracles are spectacular, which means they cause everyone who experiences them to go, "WOW!"—kind of like special effects in a movie. Only much better, and much more important.

But our wonderful loving awesome Father does many miracles every day that many people never notice! That's because His Holy Spirit is always working, everywhere in the world that His people will allow Him to.

Often we skip over some truly miraculous things because He does them quietly.

God's angels help Him in performing miracles in our lives. Those kinds of miracles may include keeping dangerous people or things away from us, and helping good things happen that are God's wonderful plan for our lives.

When the Spirit of the Lord Who is Love convinces someone that Jesus loves them so much He died for their sins then rose again, and that person believes, that is a miracle.

No person can see it, but the moment they truly believe, their spirit is moved from the kingdom of darkness into God's Kingdom of Light!

When the sweet Holy Spirit touches someone's heart and moves them to pray for someone that perhaps they haven't thought of in a long time; when He impresses them to do something like write a card with a verse for someone who may be sad or sick; these are ways He shows His glory.

Also, when He gives people the courage through His Spirit to volunteer to help in the church, somehow, or to give money to help someone less fortunate; those are all miracles of Love.

When the Holy One speaks to someone's heart and leads them to choose to be holy, which means to do the right thing, even when it's hard, that is the glory of God Who is Love!

**Now unto him that is able to keep you from falling, and to present [you] faultless before the presence of his glory with exceeding joy, To the only wise God our Savior, [be] glory and majesty, dominion and power, both now and ever. Amen** - Jude 1:24-25, AMPC

When God changes someone's thinking and helps them understand another person better, forgive them for a wrong, and love them more, that's a miracle!

When the Holy Spirit helps someone understand that God loves them so much more than they can comprehend and they are totally accepted as righteous in His sight when they believe in Jesus, that's His glory!

See, miracles aren't always "loud" or showy. Miracles happen every day. And miracles mean God's Holy Spirit is working. Miracles are the Glory of God Who is Love.

Jesus' birth was part of His glory; so is the fact that GOD would come to earth; live in a very limited human body; then suffer for all the sin of mankind on the cross; go to the world beneath and seize the keys of hell and death from the defeated enemy; then rise again.

After He rose again from the dead, He was seen of hundreds of people; and ascend to Heaven so He could send His Holy Spirit to empower all believers; these are all part of the glory of God Who is Love!

*Let's ask the LORD to open our eyes today to more of His glory; His Love, and then share Him Who is Love, with others. When we do that, He will be pleased and glorified!*

# How to Make a Resurrection Rock

This is my custom variation of a "Prayer Rock," which was a plain small stone someone gave me years ago, with a poem about the importance of prayer.

Kids (of all ages!) can make these and give to friends, teachers, family members, and even people they don't know. I've often carried them with me on trips, even to the local store, to give as the LORD leads.

People usually love free stuff, especially if it's different, and this is an easy way to sow spiritual seeds to help people know and love God!

It's also an excellent way to teach kids about the importance, power, and privilege of witnessing, while giving them a fun craft experience.

<u>Directions</u>

Gather as many small stones or buy polished ones, natural or man-made, as you want to give. Get curling ribbon, a permanent marker, and paper to print the poem on. We used plain printer paper and typed the poem below into our printer

I made several columns in MS Word, to get several copies of the poem on one 8 1/2" x 11" piece of paper, then cut them to size. You can use colored paper, and print graphics, or draw your own pictures, if you want to make it even more interesting.

Punch a hole in one corner of the poem (below), tie ribbon around it, and then tie the ribbon around the rock, or tape it to the rock.

Then take the permanent marker and draw a cross on the rock. One variation that God gave me is to draw a heart in the center of the cross—for Jesus, Who is Love, hung on that cross for us!

I also wrote a short invitation to our church and attached it.

You can modify this pattern to fit various holidays and other celebrations, for instance, "Freedom Rock" for July 4, etc.

Another variation of Resurrection Rocks was when my daughter, Victoria, and I made "Hallelujah Treats" to hand out around Oct. 31.

She was just 5 and we used the poem, the invitation to our church, and substituted candy for the rock. We assembled these, gathered a few friends, and dressed in costumes that wouldn't offend God.

Then we visited local neighborhoods, "Treating" people by giving the candy, inviting them to church, and telling them Jesus loved them.

Every one of the people were shocked and delighted—they were expecting people to come to GET; they weren't expecting anyone to come to GIVE!

These are excellent to give at convenience stores, shopping centers, your child's school parties, and anywhere you have the freedom to give.

*Get creative and make your own designs. The possibilities are unlimited! May the LORD prosper all your efforts to draw others to Him!*

(On the next page is the poem I wrote to go with the Resurrection Rocks.)

# Ressurection Rock Poem

©2012 by Tonja K. Taylor

**But he said to them, "Do not be alarmed. You are looking for Jesus the Nazarene, who was crucified. He has risen! He is not here! See the place where they put Him.**
—Mark 16:6

Jesus loves you
This is true—
He has a dynamite
Life for you!
He's your best Friend,
Your patient Boss;
He died for you
Upon the cross.
Just ask Him right
Into your heart;
That's the way
Blessed life you start.
He will with you
Everywhere
Guard your life
With loving care.

# Welcome to the Royal Family!

King Jesus will soon return to earth! He will be coming back to get all who have believed in Him, to take them back to Heaven (where there are many magnificent white horses, like in our story, "The King's Horse", in our book, *Spirit Songs & Stories Enhanced*) to live with Him forever.

The King wants to be your BFF—Best Friend Forever—and take you with Him to Paradise, where there is freedom and joy and plenty of every good and beautiful thing—and where there are no bad things, no scary things; no darkness at all.

Spirits lives forever, and Jesus created you as a good spirit who lives in a body (until your body dies), so you are already going to live forever. The choice is yours whether you live with Him in Paradise, or forever separated from Him in hell.

Every good thing in your life is from GOD, Who loves you so much that He sent Jesus (His only Son, The King!) to die for you.

King Jesus took everything you've ever done wrong and paid for your debt of sin by dying for you on the cross (John 3:16). After He was dead three days, He rose again, and He lives forever!

He wants you and every person to be His brother or sister, His friend. He wants you to say, "Yes" so you'll have a perfect life in Heaven—and to enjoy getting to know Him here on earth.

None of us can get into Heaven to live with God the Father unless we become friends with His Son. When we ask Jesus into our hearts, God adopts us as His kids!

Then Jesus is our Brother and Savior, and talks to God and reminds Him that the blood He shed for us on the cross is the sacrifice that pays for our mistakes.

At that moment, we get a perfect, beautiful new robe to wear—so that when God sees us, we look just like Jesus!

From the moment Jesus becomes our Savior, God is smiling at us!

If you would like to go to Heaven and have Jesus as your BFF, just say this prayer!

<u>Dear Jesus,</u>

<u>Please forgive me of everything I've done wrong and come into my heart and be my LORD and Savior and Friend! Help me get to know You and teach me through Your Word how to love and obey You, for You are the true King Who rules! And thank You for loving me so much. Thank You for saving me and helping me to enjoy and love You! In Your Name, amen!</u>

Romans 10:12-13 (Berean Standard Bible) says, **12 "For there is no distinction between Jew and Greek; for the same *Lord* is Lord of all, abounding in riches for all who call on Him; 13 for "WHOEVER WILL CALL ON THE NAME OF THE LORD WILL BE SAVED."**

When you prayed this prayer, a miracle just happened—you became Jesus' friend, and God's child!

The Holy Spirit also came and put a Heavenly mark on you to tell God and the angels and the devil and everyone else that you now belong to Jesus!

**21 "Now it is God who establishes both us and you in Christ. He anointed us, 22 placed His seal on us, and put His Spirit in our hearts as a pledge of what is to come."** – 2 Corinthians 1:21-22, Berean Standard Bible

The good LORD will love and help you forever!

**26 "But the Advocate, the Holy Spirit, whom the Father will send in My name, will teach you all things and will remind you of**

everything I have told you. **27 Peace I leave with you; My peace I give to you. I do not give to you as the world gives. Do not let your hearts be troubled; do not be afraid."** – John 14:26-27, Berean Standard Bible

Now Jesus and His angels are having a party for your most excellent choice (Luke 15:7, 10)!

The way to learn all about your new Best Friend Forever is to read your Bible—His special Letter to you —and ask Him to lead you to the right church family, where you can learn more about Jesus, and meet other brothers and sisters in Christ and have friends who will truly help you, and not take advantage of you nor lead you into bad things.

Also, He is the ultimate Gentleman, and never forces His will or way on anyone, so He is waiting for us to ask Him.

So you need to ask Him to help you learn to worship Him, especially in music; to pray (talk; tell Him your needs and wants) to Him; and to otherwise lead a life that brings Him glory and brings you great joy and satisfaction and success!

*Ask Him to help you with all these things, and especially to help you read your Bible daily, and to bring you the right people to help you grow in Him. He will!*

*Welcome to the Royal Family!*

Keep letting your light shine for the LORD! (Matthew 5:16) God bless you as you plant more SONflowers for Him!

The End

# Don't miss out!

Visit the website below and you can sign up to receive emails whenever Tonja K. Taylor publishes a new book. There's no charge and no obligation.

https://books2read.com/r/B-A-HSCAB-OSTRG

**BOOKS 2 READ**

Connecting independent readers to independent writers.

Did you love *How to Plant SONFlowers*? Then you should read *P.O.W.E.R. Princess Poetry Plus*[1] by Tonja K. Taylor!

Spanning decades and speaking to the depths of one's soul, the literary works in *P.O.W.E.R. Princess Poetry Plus* is for princesses from middle school to maturity and beyond. Tonja's melange of psalms, songs, and poems is a diverse and thought-provoking collection of revelatory perspectives on life--to sharpen the readers to think; to dream; to create; to envision; and to enjoy this amazing journey on earth!

**The paperback version is expanded from the ebook, and includes more songs and poems, including two bilingual English/ Spanish works, and Tonja's famous "Poet's Theorem".**

---

1. https://books2read.com/u/3njyao

2. https://books2read.com/u/3njyao

ATOS levels (www.renaissance.com) are included for every work, as well as an introduction on how to write your own poetry, songs, and fun tongue twisters!

Read more at https://www.faithwriters.com/member-profile.php?id=64826.

# Also by Tonja K. Taylor

**The Adventures of Princess Pearl, P.O.W.E.R. Girl!**
The Adventures of Princess Pearl, P.O.W.E.R. Girl!
The Adventures of Princess Pearl, P.O.W.E.R. Girl! Book III
The Adventures of Princess Pearl, P.O.W.E.R. Girl! Book IV
The Adventures of Princess Pearl, P.O.W.E.R. Girl! Book V


**Standalone**
POWERLight Lit Tips for Better Teaching
The New Legacy Expanded
P.O.W.E.R. Princess Poetry Plus
The Adventures of Princess Pearl, P.O.W.E.R. Girl!
Your Holy Health: Effective Secrets to Divine Life
Spirit Songs & Stories Enhanced
Spirit Songs & Stories #2
Visions of the King: Jesus Revealed
How to Plant SONFlowers

Watch for more at https://www.faithwriters.com/
member-profile.php?id=64826.

# About the Author

**"But when He, the Spirit of Truth, comes, He will guide you into all the truth [full and complete truth]. For He will not speak on His own initiative, but He will speak whatever He hears [from the Father—the message regarding the Son], and He will disclose to you what is to come [in the future]."** - John 16:13, AMP

We need the Holy Spirit, Who is the Truth and always tells us the Truth, every day. While there are some fantasy elements in a few of Tonja's writings, they are all based on the Truth. May they bring you delight and insight, to the Glory of Jesus Christ--Who is the Way, the Truth, and the Life (John 14:6)!

Read more at https://www.faithwriters.com/member-profile.php?id=64826.

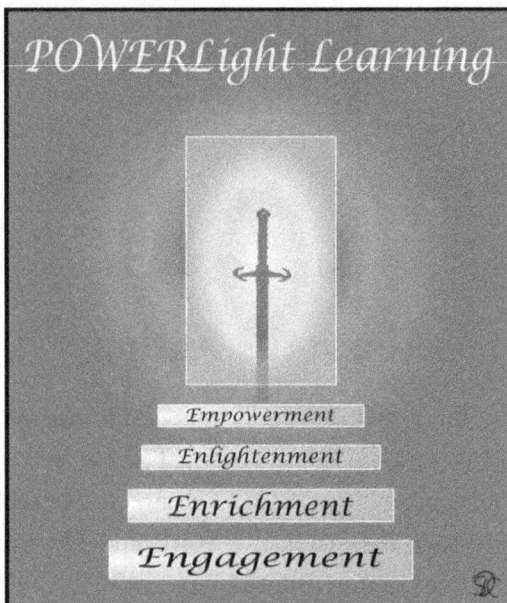

POWERLight Learning

Empowerment
Enlightenment
Enrichment
Engagement

# About the Publisher

"Do not be conformed to this world, but be transformed by the renewing of your mind. Then you will be able to test and approve what is the good, pleasing, and perfect will of God." - Romans 12:2, Berean Standard Bible

*POWERLight Learning* exists to produce writings and other creative works that engage, enrich, empower, and enlighten others about how the importance of what they experience influences their lives, and the lives of many others!

Read more at https://www.faithwriters.com/member-profile.php?id=64826.

www.ingramcontent.com/pod-product-compliance
Lightning Source LLC
Chambersburg PA
CBHW021204020426
42331CB00003B/197